The Campaign Diary of a French Infantry Officer

A FRENCH INFANTRY SOLDIER AND OFFICER

The Campaign Diary of a French Infantry Officer

During the First World War from Champagne to the Argonne, 1915

ILLUSTRATED

René Nicolas

Translated by Katharine Babbitt

LEONAUR

The Campaign Diary of a French Infantry Officer
During the First World War from Champagne to the Argonne, 1915
by René Nicolas
Translated by Katharine Babbitt

ILLUSTRATED

First published under the title
Campaign Diary of a French Officer

Leonaur is an imprint of Oakpast Ltd

Copyright in this form © 2020 Oakpast Ltd

ISBN: 978-1-78282-912-6 (hardcover)
ISBN: 978-1-78282-913-3 (softcover)

http://www.leonaur.com

Publisher's Notes

Contents

Aux grandes âmes d'Amerique qui ont si bien su comprendre et aimer la France
(To the great souls of America who knew how to understand and love France so well)

Preface of a Friend

A Campaign Diary, do you say, Reader? If the original were before you, you would not find it, like these printed pages, clean and whole. On it are the marks of war—bloodstains and smears of mud, and, from cover to cover, a hole made by a tiny piece of steel. These you may not see, but for the rest no change has been made. The author is presenting to you his notes just as he set them down at the front. The facts are true, though the form is brief, almost impersonal, and entirely without the literary flourishes that it would have been so easy to add *après coup*.

He is very young, this French officer. When the war broke out, he was still at the university, a member of that inner circle of the *École Normale Supérieure*, where he was completing his studies in literature. After the mobilisation, he qualified rapidly for an officer's commission and started for the front. His first months there were spent in the mud and desolation of that barren plain known as *la Champagne Pouilleuse*. They were months made difficult by frequent skirmishes with the Boches, and by a constant struggle with that other and more relentless enemy—the mud of Champagne.

In April, 1915, his regiment left the trenches, and crossed on foot, by daily stages, the great Forest of Argonne, all fragrant with the spring. We meet him again early in May before Arras, on the eve of the Artois offensive. Only the beginning of this offensive is described in the *Diary*. On May 9th, he fell, seriously wounded, between the French and German lines, ten yards from the enemy's trench. He himself will describe to you that terrible day and his agonising return to the French positions.

And that is all—three months of the war. It is not much, but it is enough to quicken for all time the pulse of the man who has lived it. If, among these pages, there are some that for a moment make you feel the horror and the thrill of war, then say to yourself. Reader, it is not one man alone who has thought these thoughts and endured these sufferings. It is the history of the youth of a whole nation.

L. Plantefol

École Normale Supérieure
Paris, 1917

Foreword

During the long hours of idleness spent in the trenches or behind the front, almost all the soldiers write in their *carnets de route*. And the slender notebook which they keep constantly by them is their greatest friend. It is the confidant of their troubles and their joys, of their heroism and their discouragement, which they describe naively—the reflection of their innermost thoughts. As for myself, I tried to jot down my experiences as objectively as possible, bringing together the impressions and details that counted most to me. In so far as I have succeeded in depicting only myself, may it be remembered that my ego, if it is not the centre of the world, is necessarily the centre of this journal, written without any thought of publication.

When I visited America recently, I came to realise the widespread interest in the European War shown by the citizens of the New World. To relieve the misfortunes that follow in the trail of war, they have brought to bear the great strength of their sympathy and of their material resources. But, not content with this, they give proof of a keen desire to know "just how they do things over there." And the many questions I have been asked, and the earnest attention accorded to my accounts of the war, are my excuse for publishing this journal.

I was not a soldier at the moment the war broke out; I was called to the colours in the first days of August, 1914, and went through the training for the infantry. Then my university degrees, together with an examination, made it possible for me to join a training-class for officers. At the end of this course, I was given the rank of second lieutenant on probation and started for the front.

Except for a few trifling omissions, this book reproduces exactly the notes I took at the front, though the last two chapters were written rather a long time after the events they describe—the reader will understand why. Nor is the form finished: for how shall one point phrases to the tune of grapeshot? But the story is a true one, lived and lived intensely. In this fact lies the little merit the work may possess.

René Nicolas

The Front 1915

CHAPTER 1

Arrival in the Army Zone

February 12, 1915. On the train, which at last is bearing us away to the war. My companions are asleep, wearied by a day and night of this endless journey. But I cannot sleep for joy. One thought possesses me. I am on my way to fight! If I had so wished I could have remained with the General Staff as interpreter, but what I crave is action—the intense, mad action of battle. The enthusiasm of the first days of the war has not left me, but grew greater during the long months I had to spend in training-camps, where I learned first to be a soldier, then an officer. As soon as I received my appointment to the grade of second lieutenant on probation, I asked for and I obtained permission to start for the front. Am I cherishing illusions? Is it real, this glory of war that makes my head swim?

But I am happy. The sadness of saying goodbye to my mother I have left far behind. The weight already began to lift when we made our triumphal departure from that little snow-covered town through which we marched, with the band at our head and the *Marseillaise* on our lips and in our hearts, amid the cheers of the people.

Just now the train is going through a beautiful bit of country. Never has the valley of the Saone, that I know so well, seemed so fair to look upon. Truly, *La doulce France* is a mistress we may proudly live and die for. Die? No. I have a conviction that I shall not be killed in the war; I feel sure I shall be able to do my duty to the end, and once my task is finished, return to my mother and my own life.

February 13. We have just got out of the train. I am writing in the friendly warmth of a room some peasants have put at my disposal.

This morning, in the fog and chill of early February dawn, our train stopped in the middle of a vast plain, grizzly and wet, whose monotony was unbroken except for a few clumps of trees. The bugler gave us the signal to detrain by playing our regimental march. Instantly the men streamed out, still heavy with sleep, and benumbed by these two days of travelling. I hurried to the cars of my section, lined up my men and stacked arms while waiting for orders. Fatigues were detailed at once to get rations and unload the cars.

But where were we? No one but the commander knew our itinerary in advance, for of course it has to be kept secret. We had a vague idea we were bound for Champagne. The station bore a name I did not know: Cuperly. I looked on my map and found that this village was right in the field of Châlons, several kilometres to the south of the villages of Perthes and Hurlus, which have so often been mentioned in the dispatches of late. So, we are to be launched in the midst of an offensive! What joy!

I hastily scribbled a card to my mother and gave it to a train-man, who promised to mail it.

As we stood waiting in the cold, our attention was drawn to the autobuses of a provision convoy going along the road phantom-like through the fog. And we noticed also a dull rumble like a prolonged roll of thunder. It was cannon. "Sling knapsacks! Take arms! Fours right! Forward! March!" And the battalion swung into a road that was broken up and covered with mud, a grey, filthy, liquid mud that seemed to flood the whole countryside. An artillery convoy came by and spattered us badly. It was cold.

Two kilometres farther on we halted at the edge of a village where we were to breakfast. I promptly attended to the kitchens of my section; two men from each squad went to get wood, and before long four fires were burning merrily. Pans were brought forth from their places above the knapsacks, and soon the portions of coffee and sugar provided us with a "juice" (*jus*, soldier's slang for coffee), that was much appreciated in the dampness of

14

the winter morning. I gave orders to warm some canned beef in wine for the men, and they had a real feast.

While our soldiers were resting after their meal, we section commanders, together with the other officers, accepted the hospitality of some artillery officers, who made us welcome with several bottles of champagne. The festivity was at its height when the bugle sounded. It was time to start out once again. For what destination? We did not know.

We marched two hours along the slippery road before coming to La Cheppe, where we were to await the return of the brigade that was in the trenches. We took possession of our quarters. My section was comfortably billeted in a large barn well supplied with straw, and I chose to make my abode among my *poilus*. I should like to be in closer contact with them and I am determined to make friends with them if possible. When the regiment left the training-camp I was able to procure a few little extras that they wanted, and this evening they came and invited me to dinner. The artful member of the third squad had succeeded in getting into the good graces of an old peasant woman, who gave him two chickens. The men insisted on my doing the honours, and I accepted with pleasure.

We chatted together familiarly and I told them how glad I was to be at the front, and enlarged especially on the great things I expected of them. "With you, lieutenant, we will go anywhere," said a corporal, and they all applauded. Of course, I was much pleased.

And then what a welcome the peasants gave us! My old hostess was determined to give up her bedroom to me, but I told her I would rather sleep on the straw with my men. At least I am making use of her warm kitchen where I am scribbling these lines in my diary after writing to all my family.

But tomorrow? What of tomorrow? The roar of the cannon is very loud. An attack is to be made tonight and I shall have no share in it. But my turn will come soon, I hope.

February 14. The booming of the cannon all night kept me from sleeping. However, I was snug and warm in my bed of straw beside my dear friend Henry. We are glad to be together at the war after being chums in college.

I am on duty this morning with my section. We are posted for police duty at a crossroads, and we are instructed, in addition to keeping order in the village, to regulate the movements of the convoys which pass incessantly. What an infernal whirl! Not a minute passes without something going by—a great ammunition train, heavy cannons drawn by motor tractors, a regiment of infantry returning from the trenches, muddy but triumphant. The *poilus* are radiant. We surround them. They give details. Good news! "Hot fight, all right, but the Boches are catching it like fun."

And then there go our old Paris autobuses, transformed into meat wagons. Some of them still flaunt their signs: Madeleine—Bastille, Neuilly—Hôtel de Ville, Clichy—Odéon. One is marked "*complet*," and the places, if you please, are filled by huge cattle. O valiant autobuses of Paris, you forget your luxurious existence of Parisian *bourgeois* and jolt bravely on through the mud of Champagne, accepting these hardships to save your country. We take off our hats to you in your coat of mud, for you also are doing your duty.

I went outside a moment to have a look around the village. It is very nearly intact, as it is out of range of cannon. The inhabitants are either peasants or refugees from the invaded districts. Everyone is busied in some way with the soldiers. Many have opened little shops and sell provisions, underclothing, and various other articles. Wine merchants are not very numerous, and the sale of spirits is strictly regulated. It is necessary to get permission of the officers, and they occasionally give it, wishing to improve the army ordinary.

But the commissariat is generous and each soldier receives a pint of wine a day. We officers have a special mess. We eat at the house of a peasant who has loaned us his rooms. Our cook has been a chef in the big hotels of Nice. He is excellent, and has just brought me at my post a most savoury roast of mutton.

Weather still lowering. I took out of my little chest my old volume of Rabelais and I occupy my leisure moments feasting on the exploits of Picrochole. I have brought along a few books that are easy to handle, mostly our great classics that I have been neglecting these latter years. I wish to keep up my intellectual life.

February 16. Noise of battle in the distance. Convoys pass back and forth incessantly.

This evening the battalion had manoeuvres; the men must not be left idle. Not that anyone wants to loaf. We are all burning to get into action. It is tiresome to be so near the fight and know only its echoes.

After supper I went for a walk with my friend. Twilight and absolute calm brooded over the plains of Champagne. The cold, round moon, palely reflected in the mud and ruts, cast glints as of steel. Nature, so indifferent to the deeds of men, helped us to forget them for a time, and our talk grew intimate and turned on old times as we walked along in the silence of the night.

February 17. The regiment returns today from the trenches. We are getting better acquainted with the peasants, who are the very soul of kindness. They have been telling us of their sufferings: how the Boches occupied the village,—without destroying it however, for they expected to settle there for a long time,— and then the endless files of Germans who kept calling out as they passed that the gates of Paris were open to them; finally, the return of these same Germans, shamefaced, pushed back by the irresistible thrust of our victory of the Marne. And these good people went mad with joy when behind the fleeing enemy they saw the first lines of the French with the bugler marching at the head, their native land coming back to them.

We have just inspected supplies and equipment. Each soldier has twelve biscuit, cans of "bully" beef, coffee, sugar, and bouillon cubes, without counting his own provisions, which are plentiful. The reserve supplies are sacred; they are never to be touched except under express orders. Each man has also one hundred and fifty cartridges. All these material details have been attended to, but this is not the whole of our readiness. We are also filled to bursting with enthusiasm, determination, and eagerness to fight. We start soon for the firing line.

February 19. We are ordered to go and join a different regiment; our battalion is detached and we are to fill in the vacancies made by the recent fighting. I hope I shall be able to stay with my men. It is my most earnest desire.

February 20. This morning we left La Cheppe to go to S. S. Weather dry; landscape still depressing, a desolate, muddy plain with a few scattered trees.

At Suippes we had our first real impression of war; the town is half demolished and the *château* and factories are dismal ruins—destruction wherever you look. And cannon thunder in the distance. A shell fell with a great crash on the railroad track nearby, and a great mass of earth rose slowly into the air. The Boches are very fond of aiming at this track, but their *marmites* will have a hard time stopping this enormous traffic. What an endless number of cars and sheds, what mountains of merchandise! And the procession of trains never stops.

At last we reached S. S. and came in touch with our new regiment. I belong to the Eleventh Company and command the second section. I am to keep my men. The officers received us kindly. We are lucky enough to arrive at a moment of activity, and we shall not lack work.

February 21. The village is largely in ruins. The church has been turned into a hospital. Its steeple is hidden by a covering of branches, and from a distance it probably looks to the enemy aviators just like the neighbouring trees. A little farther on was a shower-bath, which was welcome, for we were pretty well plastered with mud.

The cemetery, in the midst of the fields, is full of little wooden crosses. This evening I saw the funeral of an officer—a pine coffin followed by a bare handful of men—the regiment was probably in the trenches. A soldier-priest with the military medal on his breast pronounced the benediction.

We have no news of anything or anybody. No mail of any kind has come through yet. Shall I have to go into the trenches without receiving a single letter? I do not need encouragement, but I wish I could have had some word from home. Well, we start for the trenches tomorrow.

Chapter 2

The March to the Trenches

February 23. At last! I have just been admitted to the sacred ranks of the *poilu*; I have just had a magnificent baptism of fire, and really the Boches have done me honour. But since this journal is to be a faithful record of my campaign, I must go back a little, and follow in order the events of the last few days. Three days ago, then, we came to the trenches. Orders arrived in the morning. The captain called us together and showed us our respective positions on a map of our line of defences. Our section extended to the east of the Perthes-Hurlus line facing the north. Then after we section commanders had received final instructions, the company assembled and the captain made a short speech. Most of us were youngsters who had not yet been under fire, or else men who were wounded at the beginning of the war."

Our introduction to the first-line trenches would not give us a very complete notion of what war is really like. Our trench will be clean and well built, we shall not have to attack, and the Germans will certainly have the good taste not to bother us too much.

It remains to be seen whether these predictions were destined to be fulfilled by the events that followed.

We were to start at 5 p.m. Troops are always relieved and moved at night in order to escape being seen by the enemy and avoid inopportune bombardments. The day was spent in preparations. All the men took baths; then stocked up their haversacks and filled their canteens. They bought great quantities of canned goods; also, chocolate, condensed milk, and cigarettes. Any superfluous articles were taken out of the knapsacks and left in one of the rooms of the encampment. As the cold was sharp, mufflers were given out, and warm helmets, knitted by the devoted hands of the women of France or of America. The men then rigged themselves out after the true *poilu* fashion—greatcoats with the flaps let down, double leggings, cartridge boxes full to bursting, canteens and haversacks bulging at their hips, and above them the fringe of a long muffler ready to be wrapped three times around their necks and over mouths from which protruded the ever-present pipe. Last of all, the stick, fantastically carved, to aid in walking through the mud.

We ate early. At four o'clock I called the roll and made sure that everything was complete—food, tools, equipment—and that the guns were clean. I gave parting instructions to the cooks who were to remain at the hillock of Hurlus. Everything was in good shape. The company assembled on the road. There was a general roll-call. Beside us, the three other companies of the battalion were occupied in the same way. At a whistle from the major the companies began to move.

While we were going through the village we kept at attention and shouldered arms, but as soon as we got by the cemetery the command was given, "Route step! March!"—and then began our climb toward the enemy.

The road was appalling. It was broken up by endless convoys and covered with an abominable, sticky mud which made every step an effort, besides being very slippery. We envied the sappers of the engineering corps who, with their barbed wire and heavy tools, were sent to the front in the little Decauville railroad that runs along beside the road, and is used for carrying provisions and wounded.

We marched a long time. At the end of the first hour we made the regulation halt, on the edge of a little wood, where there was a very pretty view of the plain, dotted here and there with ruined villages.

Suddenly a terrific report right beside us gave us a disagreeable start. The captain told me it was a piece of heavy artillery twenty metres away. I looked, but could see nothing. What is more, not once during our whole march, did I succeed in making out a single piece of artillery. Inasmuch as those who pass right beside our guns cannot see them, all the more reason to hope that enemy aviators will not be able to ferret them out!

But if the big guns were not visible, it was easy enough to see the gunners, or at least such of them as were not busy with their pieces. They sat smoking their pipes at their front doors, for these gentlemen, mind you, have houses. Nicely hidden under the trees are mud huts, all covered with sod and branches. They look like the giant ant-hills depicted in natural history books, or the habitations of a Hottentot village. Stairs lead down, seemingly deep into the earth, and a peep inside that I managed to get as I passed, convinced me that this primitive form of architecture shelters a comfortable and modern interior.

We kept on marching, ever and always in the mud that plastered our shoes and flecked the bottoms of our coats with a border of grey spots that made them look like altar cloths adorned with precious embroidery. Above our heads shrieked our shells, outstripping us on our way to the Boches; and very near at hand our cannon thundered. This seemed to displease our friends the Teutons, for suddenly a great humming, as of a monster insect, grew louder and louder and came straight toward us, making everybody duck, before it finally burst two hundred metres farther on.

The first impression is not at all pleasant. The conviction is crystal clear that this snarling mass is headed straight upon you, and there flash through your mind all the tales of horrible wounds you have ever read or heard of—men blown to bits or disembowelled or what not—none of them things one is anxious to experience at first hand. Another, then another shell whistles by. Every head bobs down, while we all try in vain to hide our qualms under a smile; our nerves are not yet hardened to the fray. "Column of files!" commands the captain, and the column marching four abreast melts into four long lines, very far apart, advancing without speaking.

A few harmless shells still went by, but just as the French

seemed to be getting angry, and the detonations barked louder and louder, the Germans decided that the joke was stale, and nothing more came to make our hearts beat pitapat. However, we kept on ducking every time a shell came too near—whether French or German it made no difference—and we began to laugh every time we got a scare for nothing.

We climbed over a whole series of trenches, four or five lines, one behind the other, perfectly constructed, ready to be used in case it is necessary to fall back. The men in command are taking no chances.

After a fresh halt, the battalion formed once more by sections, four abreast, and stacked arms. We had reached the kitchens, hidden in a little ravine, and buried deep underground. Pots and pans came out of their places and were handed to the cooks. Then bread was given out, and preserves and wine. We were not to have coffee until morning in the trenches.

We set out again about 9 p.m. One more hill to climb and we should be in the communication trenches.

The battalion had been broken up and two companies only were to follow this sector, the two others going more to the east. Suddenly, down a slight incline we slid into the communication trench one by one and began to march between two walls of earth where we were entirely sheltered; it was hard to believe that we had arrived near the enemy. The night was dark and silent; no noise of cannon, only a few stray bullets that went over our heads with a sound like the swish of silk. A fine rain began to fall. After a march of about five hundred metres, the command to halt was given. We were at our destination.

"The commander of the second section," said a voice in the darkness. I stepped forward. It was the guide attached to the troops we were about to relieve who was to conduct me to my position. I received from my predecessor instructions with regard to the sector: two half-sections in separate salients, two listening-patrols, the enemy one hundred and fifty metres away, sector quiet, no casualties during the days he had spent there. But the Germans are continually on the watch, and we must be careful not to show our heads above the edge.

When I had gained this information, I asked the sergeant who was with me to go bring up the men. As my section came up on the right, the men we were replacing filed by on the left. Soon I was sole master of the field. One squad was quickly detailed for guard duty; double listening-patrols, relieved every hour, posted in shell holes in front of the trenches in the midst of the wire entanglement.

The night was very quiet, but I did not attempt to sleep. Besides, no one had any great desire to sleep without knowing the place a little better, and then the nearness of the silent enemy is a bit awe-inspiring. Just before dawn it is necessary to be doubly vigilant, for that is the critical moment; many surprise attacks, it seems, take place then. At four in the morning a messenger came from the captain to ask for a report of the events of the night. I was obliged to answer that nothing had happened.

Coffee arrived shortly, comforting and a little warm even yet. Then the day broke, cold, grey, and foggy. At last I was able to look around me.

CHAPTER 3

Life in the First Line

So, I examine my domain. It is not very extensive, one hundred and twenty metres at the most, occupied by my sixty men. My trench is composed of the communication trench and two large salients, each containing half a section or two squads. Its general arrangement is as follows:—

Each of the salients is divided in the middle by a bomb-shield, and contains therefore two squads, whose dug-outs, rather deep, are at the right and left ends of the salient. In front, in shell holes, the listening-patrols are posted during the night. There are machine-guns in each of the salients. My headquarters are so placed that I am in immediate touch with both my half-sections. A little winding trench leads to my dug-out, which is about two metres underground.

It is comfortable and contains a rather dilapidated hair mattress which the Germans, formerly proprietors of the trench, brought over from the village of Perthes. A set of shelves made of three boards has on it some old tin cans, along with the things I have taken out of my haversack. Two or three pegs stuck in the dirt wall serve as clothes hooks. The furnishing is completed by a wooden stool brought from the village, and by a brazier in which charcoal is burning. In one corner are some trench rockets and a large case of cartridges.

This domicile is not at all bad; it is almost luxurious. The dug-outs of my soldiers are large undergrounds holding fifteen men very comfortably. Straw helps ward off the dampness of the soil of Champagne and discarded bayonets stuck in the walls serve as hooks for canteens and haversacks. Meanwhile, as the cold was a bit sharp, I had some braziers made for the men by piercing holes in old tin cans with bayonets. Charcoal was brought up from the kitchens.

So, life was sufficiently endurable. We felt pretty secure. The loopholes were well protected, and one could fire comfortably. The machine-guns were always in readiness, and in short, the Germans over opposite did not seem malicious. All that could be seen of them were white streaks across the land, many and intertwined, with wire entanglements alongside. That was all—nothing that budged or had the least human semblance, only here and there a sort of ragged, bluish heap that seemed a part of the earth on which it lay—a corpse. There were not many dead directly in front of us, but to the west, on our left, much higher up, in front of the skeleton remnant of a wood, lay a number of those motionless bundles, bearing witness to recent attacks.

Thus, the region opposite us was fairly uninteresting—barbed wire, torn-up earth, skeleton trees, and dead men's bodies. And the enemy was there at one hundred and fifty metres. I discovered this rather promptly, moreover, and had a narrow escape. At a given moment, very early in the morning, I went into the communication trench that formed the eastern end of my trench. There was a large, hollowed-out place through which one could get a better view of what lay in front of us: at the left, the ruined village; in front, the labyrinth of trenches and the skeleton wood.

Suddenly, as if warned by some instinct, I turned away a little. Five or six bullets, undoubtedly intended for me, whistled through my window, one of them grazing my field-glass. Not a little shaken up, I left that dangerous spot. I soon began to laugh, however, and I should have enjoyed telling my neighbours the Boches that they had missed me. But I was more prudent after that.

Besides, everything was silent except for an occasional shell that passed high above our heads and burst so far away that we could not hear it explode. Listening-patrols, being useless during the day, were replaced by two sentries for each half-section who watched through the loopholes of the trench itself. The men in their warm dug-outs smoked their pipes, ate, read, or played cards. If this is war, thought many of them, it isn't half bad.

But, like most good things, it did not last. At nine o'clock a messenger came to tell me that the captain wanted to see me. I went to his headquarters, situated in the second line. Orders had just come. A French attack was to be delivered on the Boche trenches to the north and east of Perthes. The object to be gained was as follows: The firing line was far from being straight; as a result of the vicissitudes of the recent fighting, the German trenches made a salient into the French trenches; it was desirable to destroy this salient.

To attack at the point where we were would have been costly, for the distance between the two opposing lines was more than one hundred and fifty metres. The plan was, therefore, to attack at two other points, so that, once having taken the German trenches there, the whole system could be enfiladed. Our role was to put them on the wrong scent, and at a specified time to make as much noise as possible with our muskets and machine-guns, in order to attract attention to ourselves at the moment when the main attack was being launched elsewhere.

So, I went back to my trench and gave the men the necessary instructions. About ten o'clock we were startled by four loud reports coming almost simultaneously. It was a battery of 75's, placed two hundred metres or so behind us. At the same instant the shells went whistling over our heads and raised four black clouds in the trench opposite. It was the beginning of the bombardment. It was very violent. At the start we all ducked, but we gradually got used to it and learned to distinguish the difference in sound of the French firing. Some of the shells went by at mad speed and burst almost at once. Others took their time, especially our Rimailles, nicknamed the "ox-cart," which seems to take an airing before going to tell its tale to the Germans, and its tale is generally a terrible one.

Posted at a loophole, I watched through my glass the effect of the bombardment. All the German trenches, as far as the eye could reach, were filled with constantly recurring explosions.

EARLY TRENCH MACHINE-GUN POSITION IN CHAMPAGNE

They looked like an uninterrupted line of volcanoes. The noise and the superb masses of earth thrown up into the air fairly intoxicated me. The Boches in their turn began to answer, and scorning us poor infantrymen, sent their shells far in our rear in quest of the gunners and their guns. The chorus grew deafening. The sensation was that of being under a roof of steel, invisible but with the voices of all the fiends. And in the midst of all this din, two larks kept flitting about joyously, and mingled their song of life with the dull chant of the engines of death.

New orders came, and I sent for my two sergeants and four corporals. We were ordered to fire during exactly four minutes, from one minute past twelve to five minutes past twelve. A supply of cartridges was placed beside each loophole, so that every soldier could fire the greatest possible number of shots in the given time. All guns were inspected.

The bombardment was growing more intense, and it was no longer possible to distinguish the shots from each other. It was one uninterrupted boom, the efficiency fire that the Germans call "*Trommelfaren*," or "drumfire." For half an hour the uproar was enough to drive one mad; my head felt as if it were bound with iron and about to burst; and yet, in the midst of it all, it was a great satisfaction to think that the Boches were having to endure, in addition to the noise, the very deadly effects of our artillery. We were unquestionably better off than they.

At ten minutes to twelve everyone was at his post, and I also took my place with the second half-section. I had carefully set my watch according to the time that is telephoned every day at noon and midnight to the various officers' headquarters. At one minute past twelve the artillery lengthened its range. This was the moment, and I whistled. Immediately the guns began their clatter and the machine-guns their regular chop. At twelve-five another whistle. "Cease firing."

I had no sooner whistled the second time than half a dozen Boche 77's fell very near our trench. As there was nothing more to be done, everyone except the sentries went into the dug-outs. We were hotly bombarded, for the first six shells were followed by others and still others. This was not altogether according to our programme and the surprise was a trifle disagreeable. We had of a certainty fulfilled our mission, for we had drawn both their attention and their fire. During two hours we were deluged with shells; every shell seemed to be coming straight at us, and in spite of ourselves we shrank together and ducked, measuring anxiously with our eyes the depth of the dugout. Mine was fairly safe. I stayed in it some time with my sergeants, and we were none of us very happy.

To tell the truth, the situation is a stupid one. The role one plays is purely passive, and it is not pleasant for a reasoning human being to sit by helplessly and feel coming toward him a mass of brutish matter capable of annihilating him. Several shells fell near my dug-out. One even landed in the little winding trench that led to it, but the splinters were stopped by its turns. Otherwise, they would have made me a visit.

But I could not desert my men entirely, so I went around to the various dug-outs. Sitting huddled together my soldiers were not any more used to this kind of entertainment than I was, and would doubtless have preferred to be somewhere else; but no one was hurt, and they were glad to see me. On coming in contact with them I resumed my role of chief, and, true to the theory of William James, by pretending not to be afraid, I very soon discovered that I was *not* afraid. I chatted with them and cracked jokes, and all of a sudden, everybody felt better. Then I went back to my own quarters and made some tea on my brazier.

Shells were still raining down, but as none of them had done any harm up to that time, we bothered no more about them. They fell more especially in front of the trench, in the wire entanglement. That set me to thinking, and together with the machine-gun lieutenant I examined the situation. The Boches had battered down the parapet in several places, and the barbed wire was pretty badly damaged. Were they going to amuse themselves by attacking us? I doubled the sentries and gave orders that as soon as the bombardment slackened every man should run to his loophole.

I wondered what was up, as I did not know the result of the flank attack. I had no sooner sent word to the captain and the section commanders on either side than I saw through my glass points of bayonets here and there gleaming in the sun above the edge of the enemy's trench opposite. "Every man at the loopholes," I shouted, and in the midst of the downpour of shells every one ran to his post. Several of the men were covered with dirt by explosions, one even was knocked down by the impact of a bursting shell, but no one was hit.

Suddenly from the German trenches, like devils from their boxes, emerged the infantrymen, yelling and running toward us waving their arms. They were in close formation, three deep, I think, so that nothing could be easier than to mow them down. I quickly seized a gun and fired with the rest. The machine-guns started in immediately, and hardly more than a minute later our assailants took to flight, leaving many of their men on the ground. At fifty metres from us, forty or more Boches were lying flat on their faces as if waiting for the order to stand up. The machine-gun had done its work well. So, the assault was beaten back, but everyone remained at his post.

Wounded men dragged themselves painfully to their lines; others were groaning. No one thought for an instant of firing at them. Then, when the danger was over, came a wave of emotion. I was frightened, but the joy of having escaped a real danger made me very happy. "Now you're real *poilus!*" I cried to my men. Everybody lighted a good pipe and a bluish smoke mounted up to the God of Battles, like the incense of gratitude.

When everything was quiet, I hurried to the captain to make my report; he was well pleased, congratulated me, and instructed me to congratulate my men. Our baptism of fire had been thoroughly first-class, and we behaved rather well. During all this bombardment, only three of the company were wounded. As for the French attack, it had succeeded in seizing the extreme northern point of the German line.

The rest of the afternoon was uneventful. A few disgruntled shells came our way, but we had as an offset the thrilling sight of a splendid aeroplane reconnaissance. Six French 'planes, in a half-circle, flew over the German trenches. From time to time one of them dropped a spurt of flame into the deepening twilight, a signal for the artillery. Shells flew around our war-birds like a multitude of snowflakes that remained floating a long time in the calm air. But without paying the least attention, the aviators continued their proud flight and it seemed to us poor buried infantrymen that they were bearing aloft all our pride as Frenchmen, all our will to conquer. We were enchanted, but at the same time a little moved.

Then slowly night fell. The order came to detail two men from each squad to go with tent sheets, under the conduct of the corporal on duty, to fetch rations from the kitchens.

The trench was then organised for the night. Listening-patrols were posted out in front; it was decided that one squad from each half-section should watch at the loopholes in case of a return offensive of the enemy. About ten or eleven o'clock it was time to think of mending the barbed wire. The fatigue brought a great quantity of the Brun networks which fold and unfold like an accordion. They are very complicated and are fastened into the ground with a sort of fork.

I wanted to direct the work myself, so, accompanied by six men, I crawled twenty or thirty metres from the trench; the work went on without a word being uttered. The six rows of wire were placed one behind the other, and in front were fixed strong *chevaux-de-frise*. We were then in the midst of "No-Man's Land" near the German corpses. We heard the groans of the wounded and some little moving about, which indicated that the Germans were coming to pick up their men. But we did not make any attempt to molest them, whereas soldiers who are old in the knowledge of this war tell me that German snipers are always trying to put a stop to the work of the stretcher-bearers.

When we got back, we were rewarded by supper, consisting of sardines, roast meat, and rice, which we warmed on the braziers. After the meal I took a little rest. My two sergeants divided the rest of the night, and it was solid comfort to go to sleep snugly wrapped in my blanket, with my feet against the warm brazier. My revolver was rather uncomfortable, but it is against the rules in the first lines to disarm. At four in the morning everyone was up. Coffee arrived, ever welcome. The day was quiet;

A FRENCH FIRING LINE 1915

the Germans did not attack, but their positions were favoured with a plentiful bombardment. As for us, we were let quite alone and could sleep to our hearts' content.

The only real hardship was in not being able to wash; we were very muddy and dirty, and besides, a morning without a splash of cold water is flat and savourless; one doesn't feel really waked up. But we will get used to little things like this, I suppose.

This afternoon, everything being quiet, I invited the neighbouring section commander to come and spend a little time with me. In the trenches we rarely have anything to drink but wine and coffee, and by way of a special feast I decided to make some chocolate. So, I sent for a canteen of water, and poured some of the precious fluid into my pan and devoutly emptied in the chocolate and sugar. It was simmering gently on my brazier, and I was just on the point of adding condensed milk, when someone called me from the outside. It was my orderly coming to see if I needed anything.

I invited him to join us, but at that precise instant the stupid battery of a 77 began to spit its six shells at us. Two burst so near that my faithful *tampon* stumbled in fright and fell headlong, taking with him brazier, saucepan, and chocolate—our chocolate so nearly ready which our eyes were drinking so hungrily. The poor chap was most unhappy, so I laughed, but I must confess my laugh was a bit sickly. At that moment I detested the Germans worse than ever. It still gets dark early; my supply of candles was getting exhausted, and I wanted to save my electric lamp. And yet, I needed a light.

Then I remembered we were to have sardines for supper and the idea occurred to me to requisition the oil and pour it in an old corned-beef tin. I cut a round of cork, put a string through it dipped in oil, lighted it and behold, I had a night lamp like the ones that burn in churches. The flame was a trifle ill-smelling and rather yellow, but sufficient. I also told the cook to save me some mutton tallow. I melted it on my brazier in a tin can, stuck in a string, and this primitive candle burned very well. I gave the secret to my *poilus*.

An exciting thing happened last night. It had been snowing,

and toward one in the morning when I was chatting with the machine-gunner, the sentry outside began to fire. At the same moment a voice rang out in the night, "*Kamerad! Kamerad!*" I quickly sent up a trench rocket, and the light showed me a German soldier crawling toward us with a great clatter of tin-ware. I cried to the sentry to let him alone, and called to the man himself in German to come on. He appeared on the parapet and jumped into the trench.

I had him taken to my headquarters and there, revolver in hand, ordered him to disarm. He had no weapons but his bayonet and a belt full of cartridges, but he was loaded down with canteens. I questioned him in German. He was a great big Bavarian who had got his fill of the war. Today's bombardment—absolutely terrible, he said—had determined him to flee. He managed to be detailed for water fatigue, then made his way to our lines. He had had nothing to eat, for our bombardment made it impossible to bring up food. I gave him some bread and chocolate while waiting for supper to arrive. I kept him until morning in order to ask him certain questions, especially as to the effect of our artillery on the trenches opposite.

He told me that the attack of the day before had cost them many men, and, furthermore, pointed out without much urging the position of their machine-guns and also of a certain little revolver cannon that greatly annoyed us. This information was communicated to the artillery and since then the revolver cannon is silent. I kept the man's cartridge belt and canteens, rather good ones, and distributed them among my men. In the morning our Boche was sent to the commander. A happy man was he to have said goodbye to war.

A little later my section went to the second lines, into the dug-outs. Of the four sections of the company only three are in the first line, one being held in reserve for reinforcements. Each day we change and now it was my turn. Nothing to do. Deep dug-outs. That is where I have been writing all this long account in my notebook.

February 28. This morning I was able to wash in the snow. It is good to be clean, and I feel very fit.

The end of the day yesterday was not quiet; at four o'clock a note informed us that a German counter-attack was imminent. Vigilance and coolness were urged; our positions must be held at any cost. In case of attack, the reserve section—mine, therefore—was to go to the first line to strengthen the points attacked. I went to make sure of my fighting post and then took my men there, so that there would be no confusion in case we were needed.

The counter-attack did not come; we were heavily bombarded, but fortunately we were well sheltered and none of my men were hit; what is more, we hardly noticed the shells. The announcement came that we were to be relieved at 2 a.m.—joyful news. Say what you will, we have been through a good deal of bodily and mental strain and we have not had much sleep. Meanwhile my section is ordered to clean the snow out of the communication trenches. And then we shall return to the rear!

CHAPTER 4

Life in Cantonment and in Camp

March 3. Great disappointment on reaching our cantonment. No letters! And yet it is thirty days since I came away. We are still at S. S. in the same quarters, except that I share a room with my friend Henry; the men are well fixed and have plenty of straw. I am glad to possess a sort of home.

We were relieved at 2 a.m. The march in the snow was long and difficult. At Hurlus the battalion was re-formed and the roll was called near a wood where there was a giant masked battery—four cannons of 220 millimetres rose formidably under their veil of foliage. The casualties proved to be slight, perhaps twenty men in all. In my section everyone was present.

Then began the march through the snow. We were all so tired out by it following upon the days in the trenches that the minute we arrived and got rid of our equipment, we threw ourselves down and went to sleep.

I woke up at nine, had a bath and a change of linen, and feeling greatly refreshed, turned my attention to my men. The morning was left free and many of them slept right through. The afternoon was devoted to cleaning clothing and arms, and everyone had a bath.

I explored the village a little and found the traffic at the station particularly interesting. I chatted with several staff officers; they gave me very little information, but one of them handed me a copy of the *Matin* which I read eagerly.

But I am still tired and sleepy and I am cross at not having any letters. It seems to me it would have made up for all our hard work of the last few days.

March 4. This morning reveille at eight; review of arms and clothing—a formality quickly gone through, for the men understand that their gun is their best friend and they take great care of it. And in spite of certain accounts in the papers, the soldier is not fond of being dirty. He does not revel in his mud and filth, but suffers from it. Some of this misapprehension is probably due to the false derivation credited to the word *poilu*. It is not derived from the fact that the soldier is hirsute and unshaven. It is an old word. Under the First Empire they were the grenadiers with their bearskin bonnets, Napoleon's best troops. They called *brave à trois poils* anyone who was worthy to be a grenadier. Today the word *poilu* means simply a good soldier.

Our officers' mess is very well set up. We are going to have a special fund for extras during recuperation. The cook is nothing short of a blessing.

At last this afternoon the baggage-master announced that our communications with the rear were open. He brought us a quantity of letters; I had for my share thirty-two. *"Joy, joy, tears of joy,"* as Pascal said under slightly different circumstances.

I passed the evening with the interpreting officer, to whom I introduced myself, offering my services if he needed any help in translating documents. He was most friendly, gave me champagne, and showed me German letters and notebooks. They spoke volumes as to the state of their morale.

Tomorrow we go camping in a little wood near La Cheppe. The snow has melted, the weather is fine, almost spring-like.

March 6. In camp. The whole regiment, battalion by battalion, is gathered together in this wood. We marched to the music of the band, flag flying, into the village of B.-le-Château and reached this wood about four. Signboards on trees indicated the places of the companies. The companies were disposed in a deployed line, the sections being side by side, and in this way the ground they were to occupy was marked out. The squads of my section took their places and began to raise their tents in groups of six. Each soldier carries above his knapsack a waterproof tent sheet in which he wraps his blanket; four of these sheets make the tent proper, while the other two are used to close the openings at each end. Mine I shared with my sergeants and my orderly. Straw was given to us and the whole thing was perfect.

We had an absolute rest; nothing to do but breathe in the air filled with the fragrance of the pines, to take walks or go hunting. There are quantities of rabbits all about, and the men got up battues which wonderfully improve the army fare. The company mustered once a day, simply for roll-call and to hear orders read. But we were forbidden to go very far away, so as to be ready in case of an alarm. The regimental band rehearsing its pieces gave us pleasant concerts. To be sure, the repertory is not remarkably choice, but selections from well-known operas, polkas of Offenbach, and flute solos give a great deal of pleasure in this rough life. But some of the military marches are really beautiful, "Sambre and Meuse," for example, when the whole band and the bugler play it together.

It is full of charm, this open-air life in the country; in the evening, when it is cold, we make big fires and sit around them, smoking and chatting happily. Our morale is excellent; wine brought from the village, repose, the crackling fire, and the knowledge of duty well done—much there is to make the heart gay. I have written a great many letters. I had so many to answer. And I have read anew my *Don Quixote* with delight.

March 7. Sunday. Mass at La Cheppe, the village where we were first quartered; a little church full of soldiers, a few peasant women in black, a very old priest who spoke with sublime simplicity of the dead. I went to call on my former hosts, who were delighted to see me again. The rain made me hurry back, for the roads were already beginning to be heavy. I had to cut across lots, and even then, my shoes were weighed down with mud. The rest of the time I spent in our tent chatting, reading, and smoking.

March 8. We start for the firing line again this evening. Farewell tranquillity and the rustic life. But we go back willingly. It seems that the sector is no longer the same. The order of the day informs us that recent attacks made it possible to take the whole system of German defences in front of our former trench, which is now the third or fourth line. We are to occupy positions newly acquired.

Evening. We are making a halt for the night. It is impossible to make at one stretch the whole trip to the first lines in this mud. We started shortly after noon and marched the rest of the day in a heavy, sticky mud that is very exhausting. And the rain keeps falling, icy and monotonous. What will the trenches be like?

We are billeted for the night in a kind of little village of huts made of earth and wood, completely hidden by the trees from prying cannon, and we are passably comfortable. I have for myself and my orderly a little shanty with a place to make a fire, and a comfortable bed of pine needles. The rain is pattering on the roof. Tomorrow we return to the trenches. Cannon boom heavily. There must be fighting.

March 9. It is still raining; the soil is soaked. Our encampment is called "*Cabane-Puits*" because in time of peace it used to contain a well and a cabin. The latter is now inhabited by our brigadier-general. As for the well, it has been put in order by the engineers and furnishes water to a very large section; water fatigues are endlessly standing in line to obtain the precious fluid, which trickles in rather a tiny stream.

There is a big supply station here. The little railroad that starts from S. S. ends in the upper part of this wood, and huge sheds have been built, carefully hidden away under the foliage, in which are stored all sorts of supplies—wine, canned goods, bread, meat, straw—everything, in short, that is needed by the regiments of the brigade which occupies this sector. The traffic is very lively, and I watched the arrival of a train and the unloading and storing of the goods. I also saw a whole trainload of artillery ammunition, which is kept in very sheltered dug-outs.

Eight or ten German machine-guns, captured in the recent combats, were on exhibition. Our machine-gunners are studying them, and I too examined their mechanism; it is well to know how to use the enemy's engines so as to be able, on occasion, to turn them the other way about.

A hundred or more prisoners tramped by, looking haggard and dejected, both their faces and clothing disappearing under a mask of mud. So, things are going our way. Several wounded went by also, some on foot, others drawn by stretcher-bearers on little vehicles with springs so arranged that the men are not made to suffer unduly from jolting over these churned-up roads.

Evening. In a few hours we are going to the trenches. We are ordered to take light equipment; knapsacks are to be left in undergrounds at Hill 181, in care of the oldest man in each section. The trenches we are about to occupy are not luxurious, it seems, and the sacks would be in our way. We have been given a large supply of hand grenades. It is still raining.

French infantry machine-gun, 1915

CHAPTER 5

In the Second Line

March 15. We returned yesterday to encampment. During the last five days, the most terrible I have yet spent, I have not had a minute of physical or mental quiet to write a single line of my diary. I have run the gamut, I think, of nearly all the emotions afforded by war,—bombardment, attack, counter-attack,—all the while in a most precarious position, long painful marches through the communication trenches, and above and over all, the mud, that terrible enemy, much more terrible than the Boches. For the Boches have their moments of respite. The mud is there ever and always, implacable and relentless—the mud that keeps you from walking, chills you, clutches you, weighs you down, and drives you to despair. Five days of dragging one's self along more than knee deep in the horrible, cold, gluey paste.

It began as soon as we left *Cabane-Puits.* But at first it was bearable. We slipped, or got stuck or splashed or splattered, but that was a mere nothing. The terrible part came when we went into the communication trenches. It was fortunate that our knapsacks were at Hill 181 and not on our backs. The chalk of Champagne when combined with water rapidly forms a soft paste in which one plunges nearly up to the waist. And it was necessary to march in this; in other words, to put one foot before the other, to pull it out with enormous effort only to re-plunge it in the mire; and so on for five kilometres.

At the start, the effort was a conscious one, but at the end of the first hour the motions became automatic; all one's sensations resolved themselves into one dull pain in the whole body.

Several times I got my leg stuck, and had to appeal to the man behind me to help get it out. One of the lieutenants left his shoe in the mud; he was literally caught like a lark on a lime-twig, and when, by dint of desperate efforts, he brought forth his shoeless foot, a great laugh went round. But a little farther on we were sobered by a terrible discovery. We found the body of a soldier who had perished in the mud; he had evidently fallen while alone and was unable to extricate himself from the horrible embrace of the mire. This was the first corpse I had seen and I was much affected.

And then the tiniest of obstacles interrupted the march and upset the distances—a telephone wire getting loose from a crumbling wall, a soldier who was stuck, a fatigue coming in the opposite direction; those ahead would have to stop and the ones behind struggle to march at the double to catch up with them. A regular march was impossible.

At the end of three hours we reached the village of Perthes, or rather, the ruins of Perthes, melancholy wraith of a village, a few dismantled walls, barns that looked as if they lay in the path of an avalanche, and a church by some miracle still standing, though all ruinous. Just at that moment we were obliged to halt in the communication trench. The Boches were firing shrapnel. We huddled against the bank. I was so tired that I slept a few minutes standing up leaning on my stick. The sensation that people were moving awoke me, and once more began that slow, automatic, painful advance. A cold rain was falling, which in spite of my mackintosh trickled down my neck to my chest. Occasional spent bullets went grunting over our heads. Each moment seemed eternal.

Day broke, still overcast. We had been on the march more than four hours. Several shells burst nearby. One man had his head blown open, and remained standing. It was necessary to push this ghastly thing against the wall of the trench and nearly climb over it.

At last, after a long time, we stopped. I went with the guide to inspect my new quarters. The trench was an abomination— a charnel house—with dead piled upon dead, on the ground where you walked, above the parapets, in the walls of the trench half buried, with either their heads sticking out or their feet or their hands or their knees. We were in a communication trench that had just been seized and hastily repaired to make it tenable. I was horribly agitated, but I managed to listen to the explanations of the officer I was replacing.

We should have to use the greatest care. The trench was caught in an enfilade. Alas, our predecessors had not had a very gay time. They lost more than twenty killed or wounded. A pleasant prospect, truly. I went to get my men, and told them beforehand what to expect, so that they might be spared the worst of the shock I had had. It was not very cheering, the sight of all these dead, but our sufferings in the mud had dulled our sensibilities.

My trench, then, formed a point in the German trench. It was one of their communication trenches that we had not succeeded in seizing clear to the end. The general system of our company was in the form of a letter

At the end nearest the Germans, the trench that I was in was closed by a cave-in of earth. In front of us, the rest of the communication trench was empty up to the German trench running at right angles to our sector, and situated only about twenty or twenty-five metres beyond. At the end of the trench was the listening-post, and a machine-gun kept the Germans out of the vacant trench. Very likely their machine-guns also were ready to pepper us if we made the least move in their direction.

Thus, the situation was far from being amusing. We were caught in an enfilade, and all day long grenades, bullets, shells, and mines assailed our position. Something must be done. Two sentries were killed at their post, so I decided to use a periscope. Three in succession were shattered by bullets.

The problem was a hard one. I changed the arrangement of the sentry loopholes, making them as small as possible. I took my place there myself for a few minutes; somewhat reassured, my sentries remained on duty without flinching, beside the bodies of their dead comrades, both of whom had been shot through the eye. The Germans have gun supports to which they fasten

47

their guns and aim them at a loophole with the aid of a field-glass. After that, they have nothing to do but fire. Every shot goes home. But we managed to find a remedy for this difficulty.

There are no dug-outs, of course, and no possibility of digging any in this earth that crumbles at each stroke of the spade. I took my place nearly in the middle of the trench, on what looked like a seat that some ingenious soldier had dug in the wall. As it was rather high, I asked my orderly to dig down a little so that I could sit more comfortably. Several strokes of the pick brought to light the cloth of a uniform. I was sitting in the lap of a corpse. I went and took up my domicile a little farther on. The explosion of a shell knocked down some of the earth of the wall opposite, and in the breach appeared the green and earthy head of a corpse. From that moment, this head was my *vis-à-vis*, and once the first shudder of disgust had passed, I thought no more about it.

In the end, one gets used to living beside corpses, or *Maccabees* as we call them. They not only cease to make us uncomfortable, but they even make us laugh. Beyond the parapet there were two or three corpses, in the drollest attitudes. One looked as if he were invoking *Allah*; another was in the midst of a back-somersault. One of my *poilus* hung his canteen to a foot that was projecting over the wall; the others laughed and followed his example. The true French spirit was to the fore—an extreme adaptability, and above all, good humour.

The odour of the corpses was nauseating, but pipes soon got the better of it. Meanwhile, shells and grenades kept pouring in on us. We were obliged to use the greatest care, and keep as near the side of the trench as possible. The shells were not very dangerous when they fell in the mud, for they either did not burst at all, or they exploded without much force, but when they went from one end of the trench to the other and landed farther on, they were indeed deadly.

Toward noon a messenger came to bring orders from the captain. He was standing in front of me, halfway up to his waist in mud. Suddenly he was without a head; he tottered, but did not fall; two streams of blood spurted violently from the headless body and bespattered me. It is hard sometimes not to have the right to show feeling; my men were all around me and I did not want them to see me blanch. I simply told them to cover his body with a tent-sheet that was lying near, and sent word to the captain. These various shocks hardened me. After that, I was more or less indifferent to the terrible things that happened. I even ate with good relish in the company of the head that was sticking out of the trench. The day passed slowly, full of the anguish of explosions, to say nothing of the pain of every movement and the cold that came from sitting motionless in this prolonged foot-bath.

Night fell early. Then came orders. In the darkness a trench was to be dug, joining the two ends of our position. The men were to start at the same time from the two communication trenches and meet before daybreak. The digging was done from the trench itself, working forward as the new trench advanced. Several times corpses were turned up; the place was a regular cemetery. The work went on rapidly. The trench was to be only a metre deep and the earth was very easy to dig. But the Boches threw hand grenades, and I received for my share a splinter near my right eye. I stopped the bleeding and remained at my post. At three in the morning the crews met.

Rations arrived in very bad shape. The cooks had to make the same long trip through the mire that had cost us so many efforts. So, they brought us the coffee cold, meat all covered with mud, and vegetables that had to be thrown away. The wine alone arrived intact. Instead of its being brought in pails, I had taken the precaution to have it put in tightly stoppered canteens, the same ones the Boche was carrying when he crawled up and surrendered. Although the fatigues had slipped down several times or been knocked down by the impact of shells, the *pinard* arrived untouched, to our very great joy. Fortunately, everyone was well supplied with canned goods.

In the morning, although we were exhausted by a sleepless night in addition to the strain of all our other hardships, the order came to attack. There was a good deal of grumbling, but I emphasised to my men that if our situation was pitiable, the thing to do was to improve it. It was to the interest of all of us to go across the way, where we should certainly be more comfortable; and the attack would not be dangerous. We should dash to the assault from the trench dug the night before, at a moment when the Boches did not expect it, and there would be so little ground to cover that the risk would not be great. Besides, it was our duty, and I was certain my *poilus* would keep the promise they had made me to follow wherever I led.

At two o'clock the whole company was to take its place in the new trench; at 2.10 we were to make the attack. However, things did not happen according to schedule, and the Germans gave us the opportunity to take their trench almost without any losses on our own side, but with many losses on theirs.

Toward eleven o'clock, when our bombardment had only just begun, our machine-guns began to clatter and likewise all the guns at the loopholes. The Boches were attacking! They had a hankering after the trench we had dug during the night, and wanted to launch an assault on our lines from that point—the exact thing that we were planning to do to theirs. They came on in full force, but there was time for the machine-guns to mow down numbers of them before the first ones reached the new trench. The mud kept them back, and the poor wretches made a tragic struggle to get their feet loose and to hurry. Three successive waves started. The machine-gun at the end of our trench was quickly shifted, and enfiladed our new trench full of Boches, killing nearly all of them.

It was horrible but magnificent. But others were coming on. Then I commanded, "Fix bayonets! Forward! Forward!" and we dashed against the assailants. The whole company followed my example and rushed forward. Was it to be a hand-to-hand fight? Our murderous grenades crushed the first row, and in the face of our air of determination the others hesitated, then turned tail. We threw grenades at them and fired at close range. We kept sticking in the mud and stumbling over bodies, but the opportunity was too good to be lost. We followed them home; their batteries and machine-guns could not fire for fear of hitting their own men.

They had no sooner reached their trenches than we were at their heels, stopping just long enough to shower in grenades before we jumped in after them. I had a feeling that someone was aiming at me and I emptied my revolver point-blank into the head of an *oberleutnant* who was wearing a monocle. I did this automatically, by reflex action. I seized another enemy by the throat and struck him in the face with the butt of my revolver. He fell like lead. But the hand-to-hand fight did not last long. The forty soldiers who were left quickly surrendered.

"Quick! Quick!" I commanded. "Reverse the trench!" In other words, pierce several loopholes and turn the German machine-guns against their own trenches. We stopped up the communication trench, and opened up the ones toward the rear, and the prisoners filed through my former trench, which was once more a communication. We then prepared to ward off the counter-attack. Barbed wire was brought and securely fastened. The Germans proceeded to treat us to reprisal fire, which damaged our newly conquered trench rather badly, but did little real harm.

I lost nine men in all, four killed and five wounded. The Germans had been neatly outwitted. By quarter-past eleven we were established in our new positions. These events had lasted but a very few minutes—the hand-to-hand fight just long enough to let me kill two Germans.

Nevertheless, the situation was none too cheerful. German corpses were all about. Our grenades had done their work well, and any wounded were drowned in the mud as they fell. As we walked, the bodies sank in deeper, for the bottom of the trench was literally covered with them, forming a sort of carpet under our feet. In spite of it we were radiant. The commander expressed his satisfaction. The counter-attack might come at any moment, but we were ready for anything; as for shells, we laughed at them. Everyone gathered trophies. I carried off the revolver and field-glass of my *oberleutnant*, also his notebook, which I proposed to decipher and hand over to the staff officers.

Night fell gradually. The air was very sharp, and it began to rain again. We all looked like Capuchin friars with our blankets wrapped around us and our tent-sheets over our heads. No one could sleep, or rather, no one was allowed to sleep; but as I made my way with great difficulty back and forth in the trench, I saw several men asleep, holding their guns at the loopholes. In order to keep them awake I made them fire salutes. The bombardment was intense all night, but it was directed more especially against our second lines. That augured a counter-attack for the next day. At midnight word was sent that we should be relieved at 2 a.m. Great rejoicing. At last we should be able to get some sleep! Quickly we folded blankets and tent-sheets, but we had a long wait in the rain that was falling and under the shells that were dropping.

It was not until daybreak that the others came to relieve us. And then began anew the fight with the mud. It took us nearly two hours to reach Perthes. There we learned that we were not to be sent to recuperate, but were to reinforce the third line in the fortified dugouts of Hill 200. Then we left the communication trenches, for they were in too bad a state, and walked in the road, almost in the open. A rather high parapet protected us from bullets and from being seen by the Germans, who were about a kilometre to the north. But we had to march bent double, alternately making rapid leaps and stopping. Of course, a few bullets came our way, but the Boches did not see us and we were not molested. Once when we stopped, I saw stretched out in the road beside me a dead soldier, with his pipe still in his mouth. Evidently, he had not suffered much.

After five hundred metres on the road we had to go into the communication trench again; that is to say, begin to flounder through the mire. A big German shell had fallen into the trench without bursting, and we were obliged to climb over it. Dangerous engines those, that a mere trifle may cause to explode. I wonder now how we managed to keep going for another hour, for it seemed at every step that we should sink in our tracks. It had been impossible to send up rations, and we had nothing to drink. Some of the men suffered so from thirst that they scooped up in their hands the muddy water that was lying stagnant in the trench and quaffed it with delight. I had a flask of mint and I drank a swallow that refreshed me greatly. We were so tired at the last that we could neither see nor feel, but stumbled on with our eyes shut, some of the men asleep as they went. At last we arrived.

These dug-outs were a sort of cave made in the side of the hill, large galleries well propped up with planks with the entrance carefully protected by a regular rampart of bags of sand. The minute we arrived we threw ourselves down and slept and slept, in spite of the big German shells that were bursting with a frightful hubbub, and in spite of a French battery concealed nearby that kept up an incessant fire, and in spite of our consuming thirst. We didn't wake up until the commissary arrived, bringing letters and rations. Everybody demanded the letters first. We were in such sore need of a few words of endearment, much more so than of food! I got for my share five letters which I read hungrily. I also got a package of eggs my little godmother managed to send me from Lorraine, and they were a wonderful feast, sweet as a caress of the one who sent them.

Then we ate, and went to sleep again. We cannot be entirely brutish, since letters bring us such joy. We have killed men, under penalty of being killed ourselves, and also because it was our duty, but these combats took place in a sort of frenzy, the frenzy of action, of enthusiasm, and likewise of suffering. I have killed two Germans and I am proud of it, and yet, I have not the soul of an assassin.

At eight in the evening the major received word that two companies were to be sent to the trenches. All the troops were jaded, all had laboured long and hard; we drew lots—Eleventh and Twelfth. So, I had to set out again. I went to rouse my men. They grumbled a little, but obeyed philosophically, buckling on their equipment and folding their blankets. At nine o'clock we set out to traverse in the opposite direction the ground we had come over in the morning: trench, road, trench, village, trench, mud, and again mud. It was impossible to maintain distances. One section got lost and had to turn back; then troops were met coming the other way, the ditch was narrow, and it was slow work squeezing through.

Order was once more established as we came near our goal.

The night was full of the uproar of a battle. Machine-guns were emitting in the distance the regular *click* of a sewing-machine, while the little guns sounded like the sputtering of fish in a frying-pan. A few bullets whizzed by. I heard one of the men say, in his utter weariness, "I hope one of those bullets is for me." I chided him mildly, but it was exhaustion that wrung this cry from him, for the day before at the moment of the attack he had fought with the bravest.

We arrived at an empty second-line trench that we were to occupy, and defend in case of need. But it was very different from having the enemy right before us, and we could be comparatively tranquil. We went to sleep sitting in the mud, or in the dug-outs, where the brittle earth crumbled and fell in tiny frozen pellets. We slept the rest of the night and spent the following day almost without moving, wearily awaiting the moment to depart. We were disgustingly dirty, caked with mud from head to foot. We scraped the mud off our hands and faces with our knives; our hair was converted into a strange, unfamiliar substance that looked as if it would withstand any process of cleaning.

A few shells fell among us, and several of the men were wounded, but we were perfectly indifferent and didn't budge when the explosions came. The *marmites* were not honoured by us with the slightest attention. Although we were physically tired, our morale was intact, and the men laughed and joked, every one recounting the deeds of prowess he had performed at the time of the attack. Who shall blame us if we were a little boastful? We were tasting the satisfaction of work well done. If the Boches had chosen that moment to attack us, they would have had a warm welcome. However, they didn't risk it.

Toward eight in the evening orders came that we were to be relieved. They were greeted with a satisfaction not unmixed, for no one smiled as the prospect rose before him of the return trip through those communication trenches. Slowly, with many difficulties, and at the cost of great efforts, we made our way once more through the mire. We were simple automatons with very little more notion of time and space than a pendulum on the end of its pivot.

We reached Hill 181 and solid ground, solid except for big shell holes filled with water. A number of the men, blind with fatigue, fell into them and had to be pulled out with rifle butts. Shells were falling, so we changed into open formation to march the five hundred metres that separated us from the kitchens. Hot coffee awaited us there, but we could not stop long enough to drink it, as shells were coming down too fast. It was not until some distance farther on when the coffee was cold that we were able to refresh ourselves. The Germans were keeping up a continuous bombardment of *Cabane-Puits*, so that we could not stay there, but had to go to B.-le-Château, twelve kilometres beyond.

The long column of the regiment wound through the plain four hours longer with numerous halts and untold weariness. The knapsacks that we had picked up again dragged heavily on our shoulders. From time to time, exhausted men left the ranks and lay down in the road, falling asleep with their packs on their backs. We were very near the end of our tether when the cock on the steeple appeared at a turn of the road. A long halt was made here, and the stragglers had time to regain their places before we marched into the village. Was there such a thing as being able to shoulder arms and march at attention in our state of exhaustion?

Yes indeed, and it was sublime. The colonel, before dismissing us to recuperate, wished to have us file before our flag, our beloved flag, blackened and torn by battles. We had earned this honour, and it made us forget everything else. Every man of all the mud-smeared ranks felt that his very soul was wrapped in the glory of that sacred emblem for which he had suffered so much and so willingly. Now as a supreme reward, while we still bore upon us the marks of duty well done, we were to perform in the presence of the flag an immense and joyous act of faith in our native land.

All the men felt the solemnity of the moment; and to the ringing notes of the farewell hymn that tells us to live and die for our Republic, these worn and footsore men, so covered with grime as to have scarcely a human semblance, defiled before the flag and presented arms as they never had presented them before. And when I saw my men stand up proud and straight to present arms, putting into this act all the little strength that was in them, and when it came my turn to salute our colours, I was so stirred that the tears rolled down my mud-stained cheeks. I am happy. I give thanks for all I have suffered, since it has won for me the joy of this moment.

CHAPTER 6

In the Fourth Line

And then we went off duty. I was determined to be clean before I went to bed. A soldier employed at the bath-house was obliged to scrub me all over with a stiff brush. Not a spot on my body had escaped the treacherous mud. We had two days to rest and clean up and put our clothing and arms in order. The men were allowed entire freedom.

My billet is comfortable. I even have a real bed—a bed with sheets—that I share with my friend H. Joy and delight to be able to take off one's clothes and crawl into bed between sheets—a luxury we have not tasted for a month. And such a month!

This morning there was drill. Not very interesting, but according to theory, the men must not be left idle. I suggested that we organise games and the idea was approved. Peace-time manoeuvres afford little amusement to men who are just back from the trenches.

Our mess is very jolly. We officers get together and chat, play cards or have music. I often go and play the little organ in the church. A priest who is on the hospital nursing staff has asked me to play during services. I consented with great pleasure. There is a service every evening which many soldiers attend. They sing the hymns of the liturgy. I accompany and I amuse myself playing some fugue of Bach or of my beloved Cesar Franck. The organ is nothing to boast of, but I get a good deal of satisfaction out of it.

March 18. We start tonight for *Cabane-Puits* which forms the fourth line of our positions. We are not to go to the trenches, it seems, but will remain four or five days in reserve. Furthermore, we shall be assigned fatigue duty. My company is flag escort.

Evening. We left B.-le-Château toward noon. The ceremony of departure was beautiful. The third battalion had the flag and my company was chosen to escort it. The battalion formed in line of masses, my company being posted directly in front of the colonel's house. At noon, bayonets were fixed, and at the moment the flag appeared on the threshold the band and the buglers saluted and played the *Marseillaise*, while every man presented arms. We defiled through the village with the flag in the middle of the company, just behind my section. Then the flag was folded into its black sheath, and we began the march.

The road was better, much better. We met a regiment coming back from the trenches, and it made us realise what we ourselves had looked like a few days before.

Cabane-Puits is very curious—a village of primitive tribesmen made up of half-buried huts of earth and branches. These dwellings are very comfortable, however, with their fireplaces and thick beds of straw. There are also dug-outs for each section. For myself I have a private apartment which has been comfortably arranged by its various occupants. There is a bed made of woven wire hung like a hammock about twenty inches from the ground, a rough table, shelves, and a fireplace of big stones. The baggage-wagons of the regiment have come with us up to this point, so I have my chest and can profit by my books. Rabelais and Montaigne have promptly been given the place of honour on the shelves.

There is a shanty for everything here. The infirmary is very well installed; the offices of the various companies have packing-boxes for desks. The kitchens are in the open air. Above the fires, hanging on a stick, great kettles boil and bubble everlastingly. We had tea this evening, but sad to say, there wasn't enough sugar. Letters come through with more or less regularity. I have made friends with the baggage-master, who scolds me all the time for being one of those who give him the most trouble; for I have a correspondence of almost ministerial dimensions.

Take it all in all, this is better than the trenches.

March 19. A delicious existence. Weather fine. Nothing to do. I read a little, write a little, chat a great deal with my friend H. or with the *abbé-infirmier*, a man of extraordinary intelligence and a heart of gold. Last evening after going to bed, H. and I lay awake a long time and talked, with the splendour of the spring flooding in upon us. The cannon in the distance were raging, and in spite of ourselves we rejoiced in our comparative security. "*Suave mari magno.*" ("Sweet it is when the winds are ruffling the mighty surface of the deep to witness the grievous peril of another from the shore.") Perhaps Lucretius was not so far wrong. But this kind of selfishness is conceivable when one thinks of the sufferings of the week just past.

March 20. A very busy night. My section was detailed to clean out the communication trenches near Perthes. The mud had dried and filled them in so that they were no longer deep enough.

We started at 9 p.m. along Hill 181. At the entrance to the trenches, sheltered behind a hillock, are the headquarters of the commander of the sector, and likewise a tool-house. Picks and shovels were piled up waiting for us. We took an equal number of each alternately, and proceeded to the trenches. A guide showed us the way. They were in a very bad state from the point of view of protection, but oh, so easy to walk in. The sector we were to put in order was about two hundred metres long. With the aid of my sergeants and corporals, I measured off the exact space for each pair of men. Everyone set to work with a will, and at the end of two hours the job was finished.

Partly to keep warm and partly to set the example, I took a pick and worked here and there. We deepened and broadened the trench and put bomb-shields every twenty-five or thirty metres, so that a bursting shell could be effective only on a limited area. Moreover, the trench was wide at the bottom, and the walls were near enough at the top to give less purchase to shrapnel. I had the satisfaction of feeling that the work had been done rapidly and well. At 1 a.m. we arrived at quarters. I gave the men a swig of brandy to warm them up, and we all turned in.

An enemy aviator was brought down this morning. He ventured near our lines and was subjected to a lively bombardment. Swarms of white tufts circled and unfolded around the 'plane, which made a yellow spot in the lens of my field-glass. Suddenly I saw it dip, nose downward, and dart like an arrow to the ground. Meanwhile the smoke of the shell that had done the deed spread majestically through the sky as if content with its handiwork. The aviator fell too far away for us to go and see him.

The Russians have taken Przemysl. The news was announced in this morning's bulletin. It seems the booty is enormous. To celebrate the event every soldier has been given an extra ration of wine.

It is one of the first bits of war news we have had. We are narrowed down to our own sector, and know practically nothing of what is happening outside. Not much probably. But surely something will be doing before long now. Everyone thinks the grand offensive will take place in the spring—the decisive blow that will pry the Germans out of their holes in the ground and bring us the fight in the open for which we are all longing. And then—victory!

I find myself yielding to the charm of our life here. It is, indeed, the return to nature and simplicity; it is almost physical, almost animal. The primitive instincts of the race have full sway—eating—drinking—sleeping—fighting—everything but loving. Lacking this, Rousseau would have found his idyll complete. But however, much we are sunk in savagery, memory still is living. As well ask the spring not to be green as keep one's thoughts from wandering among cherished images, kept fresh by almost daily letters. Beloved little godmothers, precious are your letters and welcome your delicate gifts to those who fight. We are glad to fight for you. But at times, the thought of you makes the chains of war very hard to bear.

However, I am determined not to let my mind grow rusty. I read a great deal, write quantities of letters, and I have two or three friends with whom I can converse intimately. What is more, I have a most interesting study in psychology always close at hand—the study of my *poilus*. I think I am beginning to know them better and to be their friend; they tell me their secrets and

An Uphill Attack

their adventures, their little family affairs and their love affairs. Some of them want me to read their letters, or show me photographs. All this makes it easier to approach each one of them in the right way to make him do his best. I have grown very fond of them, for they are fine fellows; they can even be heroes when duty requires.

I passed the evening out of doors, lying sprawled in the grass, smoking my old pipe, companion of all my adventures, and chatting with my friends. The sound of the cannon was scarcely audible, and over the unruffled air came whiffs of music. We recognised the "Russian Hymn" and the "*Marseillaise*" and "God Save the King." It was a regiment encamped behind us, celebrating the fall of Przemysl.

It is late. I have loitered outside in the marvellous night, keeping company with the spring. The air is laden with perfume as I write. But "*Sat prata biberunt.*" ("Fields have drunk.")

March 21. Sunday. This morning mass was said in the open air behind a great rock, a soldier priest officiating. Stones served as an altar. On it were two candles without candlesticks—an old-time simplicity. The gathering was large, and we sang canticles to the deep accompaniment of the distant cannon.

Nothing has happened today, except that a few prisoners filed by.

This evening several men of the company go on fatigue duty to carry wire and shells to the trenches. I examined the shells. They have tiny wings and are fired from a cannon in the trench itself, and are very deadly, it seems. Our *poilus* call them "cauliflowers."

My section is on duty, for of course we have to take turns keeping guard. The service is very simple. Three sentries suffice, one near the station and storehouses, one near the colonel's cabin where the flag is, and the third near the carriages.

March 22. Another uneventful day. The battalion had manoeuvres in the woods. If only this gives promise of the fight in the open! A little alarm—several shells fell on our position. A kitchen was destroyed and a cook wounded. It is very unpleasant to be bombarded when you are off duty. In the trenches, it is part of the day's work, and for that reason swallowed down cheerfully. Besides, the trench is a protection, but in encampment where, by the very definition of the word, one has a right to feel secure, it is annoying. Those Boches have no manners.

March 23. Last night I was detailed with half my section to bury the dead. The task was not a pleasant one, but it was accomplished without reluctance or hesitation. Having to do the work at night made it a shade more lugubrious. A guide conducted us to a little thicket all laid bare by grapeshot, south of Perthes and about three kilometres from the first lines. There was no moon, and it was very nearly pitch dark. Trench rockets streaked the sky here and there, and from the distance came the crack of musketry. Shells went labouring by with the heavy breathing of wild beasts in a rage. A little trench was made into a large one to receive the bodies, and then we set out in search of them. They had been lying there for a very long time, and it was only the recent advance of our lines that made it possible to bury them.

With some difficulty we managed to make out these motionless heaps on the ground. It was necessary to search the pockets and take out papers, money, etc., also to unfasten the identification badges that are worn on the arm like a bracelet. It was not an easy thing to do. In this, also, I was obliged to set the example. I had to put my hand into the pockets of a foul mass that fell to pieces at a touch. I found nothing but a pocket-book and diary. The men then took courage and overcame their aversion. The bodies were not offensive until they were disturbed, but the least jar brought forth an odour that choked you and took you by the throat.

Among them were three Germans. They were all carried in a tent-sheet to the trench and laid side by side. The articles found on them were kept carefully in separate packets. Out of twenty-seven, we succeeded in identifying all but three.

When our task was finished, the *abbé-infirmier*, who had accompanied us of his own accord, stepped to the edge of the grave and said a blessing. And that priest, standing out against the darkness, lifting his voice above the noise of battle in a last solemn duty to those pitiful fragments, was truly very fine. Every man of us, whether moved by religious conviction or not, felt the impressiveness of the moment, and knelt to hear the words of forgiveness and of life.

This evening I went to S. S. by the little train to have the death certificates made out. The tiny mementoes had to be sent to the families—letters, purses, notebooks, watches. On one of the bodies was a letter bearing the inscription:

> Will the person who finds my body have the kindness to send this letter, together with the exact description of my grave, to the following address. . . . .

I took the letter, and wrote a few words to the family. I did my best to make a drawing of the spot where the poor fellow was buried, and told them about the blessing that had been said over his grave. And into the same envelope I put that sacred letter, bloody, smeared with mud, ill-smelling—a letter from the dead.

March 24. An artillery officer who was at the village with me yesterday invited me to go and see his battery. After the daily muster of the company I started out. I had marked on my map the exact position of the battery and found it without difficulty.

The captain received me in his dug-out, a regular palace compared to the squalid quarters of us poor infantrymen. Twenty feet underground, well supported by planks, it contained all sorts of modern comforts—a real bed, a table, chairs, besides a quantity of knick-knacks that indicated a prolonged stay. Pinned up on the walls were the delicious women of Fabiano, of Nam and of Préjelan, taken from "*La Vie Parisienne*"; a violin was hanging in one corner, and on a table lay the sonatas of Bach. There were a number of little objects on the shelves made from fragments of shells. My host gave me tea in china cups.

All this luxury enchanted me. A telephone on the table connected the dug-out with the battery, the first line, and the colonel's headquarters. I could not resist asking him to play, and this pupil of the Polytechnic executed for me, and executed well, the famous saraband.

"Now, after the chamber-music," said he, "I'm going to let you hear the grand orchestra." And he conducted me to his battery. The four pieces, all draped in foliage and well covered with earth, were silent. But they remained fixedly aimed at their invisible objective, a trench some three kilometres ahead. Thanks to the hydro-pneumatic brake, the 75 does not need to be re-aimed after firing. To please me, the captain ordered three shells fired from each piece. I even fired a shot myself. Finally, I saw the little valve that has only to be manipulated in a certain way to render the piece useless in case it falls into the hands of the enemy. The gunners are under orders to attend to this.

I took leave, with many thanks to my host for his kindness. I was gratified to have penetrated a little into the sumptuous domain of the artillery.

On arriving in camp, I learned that the captain had sent in my name for promotion to the rank of second lieutenant, because of what happened last week. I am very much pleased.

March 25. This morning to our great surprise we were told to return to S. S. We reached there toward six o'clock. Same quarters as before. I noticed in passing how rapidly the cemetery has been growing of late.

March 26. Review of our brigade this morning. The two regiments assembled by sections in columns of four, with flags and music. The general passed along our front at a gallop. Then we defiled. The impression of strength is immense when one stands in the midst of all these glittering bayonets above which float the bright colours of our flag—the wall of steel that is holding back the enemy and will crush him when the hour strikes. With it all comes the consciousness of one's own role, which is humble and yet great. For that wall of steel is made of glittering, separate points, and I am one of them. It is joy untold to be able to say to one's self, "All my struggles and all my sufferings count for something in the great action of the whole."

The general then went along by the different companies. He stopped to speak to me, and told me that from today I shall rank in the army as second lieutenant.

Naturally, this event had to be celebrated. I treated my colleagues to champagne. Just as festivities were well under way, orders came to start at once for the trenches. Here is the programme for the next few days:—

Two days in the first line.

Two days in reserve, Hill 181.

Two days in the second line.

It is rumoured that this army corps is to be laid off a whole month to recuperate.

Lots of rumours float about, fantastic and otherwise. It's what they call "kitchen gossip." But this one is perhaps true. Meanwhile we are buckling on our things, and in two hours, off we go.

I am going to write to all my people to announce my promotion.

CHAPTER 7

Our Last Days in Champagne

March 27. I am writing my journal in a big underground shelter, comfortably stretched out in a hammock that someone has rigged up of two old tent-sheets. We are in an ugly sector, and are using the mine galleries as dug-outs, for grenades are falling thick and fast.

We are in the same trench as the enemy—next-door neighbours in fact, and not a bit civil. Nothing but a barricade of bags of earth separates us from the Boches. Near the barricade stand the sentries, attentive and silent. No sound is heard on either side except for the whizzing of grenades that are continually being tossed back and forth. But the sentries are well protected in the sides of the trench, like saints in niches, and they defy the German "turtles."

The first German and French lines are in immediate contact. The reason is that our side has not been able to seize the whole of the trench, of which the enemy still occupies the eastern end. But this situation will not last, I think, and we shall increase our gains.

The trench is clean, except for bodies imperfectly buried here and there. We no longer pay any attention to them, but the really deplorable thing is that many corpses fell in the mud, the mud has hardened, and the trench is less than five feet deep. It is impossible to make it deeper, for the least stroke of a pick brings up a piece of cloth or a bit of flesh. To move about, we have to bend like hunchbacks. It is both painful and dangerous, so the men don't move around much but stay in the shelters.

There is something very amusing here—a trench cannon, a Little one such as people fire during popular celebrations. You put powder in it, then a 77 shell (German projectiles that get sent back to them), then a fuse that is lighted with a tinder—noise—smoke—the shell goes off in one direction, the cannon in the other. The little fiend ought to take lessons of the 75's to cure it of going on its dance after each shot. But there is plenty of time to re-aim, and a man especially detailed for the work takes charge of it. Of course, I couldn't resist firing it a few times. The pedestal is gruesome. It is a corpse, a body well encased in mud, except that the feet are sticking out. It is a Boche.

The soles of his shoes are shod with iron just like horseshoes. This fact has caused a good deal of merriment. The shells are sent to the trenches over opposite. For the German trench at our side we use hand grenades, and not stingily either. They too, of course, are making the best of their opportunities, though up to now we have no wounded. But we have had some unpleasant escapes from being overcome by gas. The Germans vary the monotony of the missiles that come over the barricade by sending gas bombs. These bombs in bursting emit an acrid smoke that smells of sulphur and fills the whole trench. We discovered that we could ward off the worst of the danger by putting handkerchiefs before our mouths. When these bombs burst against the wall of the trench, they leave a yellow splotch.

I remain quiet very little in the trench. I have a horror of inactivity, and I don't seem to want to read, so I wander back and forth a good deal from one end of my sector to the other, keeping an eye on everything.

A little while ago one of my *poilus* came to me and said: "I think, lieutenant, the Boches are busy mining our trench." I listened but heard nothing. Then I went into his shelter and I did, for a fact, hear muffled blows, struck regularly. Evidently, they were working underneath us. It is very disagreeable when you are already underground to feel this hidden, slow work, impossible to prevent, that may blow you up at any minute. And the tiresome part of it is that since that moment, everyone is convinced that he hears the strokes that are digging the abyss underneath him. Such is the power of imagination, Pascal.

But the captain was notified and telephoned in turn to head-quarters. An officer of the engineering corps came and listened with a microphone, and said we were in no danger; in the trench beside us a French mine gallery has already been pierced underneath that mine. In front of all the network of trenches there are underground listening-posts where the sappers listen with their microphones and register the least sound. This officer told me that two days before he had blown up a Boche mine. In order to do that, the exact location of the enemy's gallery must be ascertained, then a hole is bored toward it with a drill similar to the one used in boring wells.

When the right spot is reached, it is packed and blown up with a bickford. The explosion chamber of the German mine goes into the air along with its inhabitants. The same fate awaits the mine we have been worrying about. In mine warfare, the essential thing in the conflict is just the opposite of the war in the air, where it is a question of getting above the enemy aviator. The counter-mine, on the contrary, must go beneath the enemy mine; when it reaches it at the same height, they blow it up. It sometimes happens that the miners suddenly find themselves face to face with the enemy. Then they kill one another as best they can, with hammers if they have no revolvers.

It is not very edifying, this kind of warfare. I am going to console myself by inviting my sergeants to tea.

For the fun of it, I have concocted a letter and thrown it into the Boche trench beside us. In my most polite German I invited those who were tired of waging war to come and surrender. They would be well treated by the French. They would simply need to present themselves, *unarmed*, in front of the barricade of bags of earth and whistle the first measures of a tune known to all Germans, "*Ich hatt' einen Kameraden.*" In a little while the sentry brought me a paper. It was the answer. Here is the translation:

We shall be relieved tonight about one o'clock. We will take advantage of the confusion to come, three of us together, and surrender. At midnight we shall be on sentry duty near the barricade. We count on your promise to treat us well.

I carried this paper to the captain and translated it to him. The information as to changing troops was interesting; he is going to telephone it to headquarters.

March 28. What a riotous night! And by the same token, what a good piece of work we did! We took all the trench beside us, about fifty metres, and a machine-gun.

The first part of the night was uneventful, except for an abominable shower of grenades the Boches kept basting at us. Three of my men were wounded, slightly, I think, for they were able to walk to the dressing-station. About half-past ten the captain came to look over the situation, and I suggested that it might be a good idea to attack the trench at the moment they were changing. The various possibilities were considered, and finally my superior officer told me to do as I saw fit, leaving me the entire initiative in the matter. All I asked of him was to forbid the second line to fire.

I sent for my friend H. and entrusted to him the command of my section after carefully discussing the various contingencies. The most devoted and intelligent of my corporals was to go with me, and I called for volunteers from the squads to help in an undertaking that might prove dangerous. Almost all the men offered. I chose six, who armed themselves with their bayonets, and took ten grenades apiece. Then I went to the barricade and, with the aid of a periscope and trench rockets, was able to get an exact idea of the German trench. One thing bothered me—a machine-gun placed not far from us. I ordered a score or so of grenades thrown at it. Men were hit, but the gun seemed intact.

Shortly after eleven o'clock I heard them whistling the popular air of the *Uhlans.* I whistled it in turn, when presently three great gawks appeared on the barricade with their arms raised above their heads, and jumped into our trench. I put them under strong guard and questioned them. It seems their comrades were leaving at that very moment; they were being sent away before the arrival of the other troops. These three had managed to be put on sentry duty and at that moment no one was guarding the entrance to the trench. For a second the idea flashed through my head that this was a trap, and I threatened to have them shot if they were lying.

But I went to the barricade and saw that the trench was for a fact empty, except for the machine-gunners who were on duty beside their gun. I quickly gave orders to tear down the barricade and we ran into the Boche trench. The men of my section, according to my instructions, set up a furious fire in order to distract the attention of the enemy from the sector we were trying to take. As we ran, we threw grenades at the machine-gunners, who sank down before being able to turn their guns against us.

In a twinkling we reached the end of the trench, intersected at right angles by a communication trench. A few grenades went after the last Boches who were going off to recuperate. Like lightning we piled up four or five bodies and rolled down several bags of earth from the parapet, brought up the machine-gun, and from behind the barricade of dead men and earth fired three rounds into the retreating Germans. They were thrown into a panic. A good many must have been killed, for daylight disclosed to our gaze that trench piled with dead. The whole thing had not lasted more than two minutes. We were deluged with grenades, a continuous *zip, zip*; one of our men was killed, three or four wounded.

Everything was in a wild tumult—trench rockets going up, guns firing at the double-quick, a hasty report to the captain who came to shake hands with me. Barbed wire was rushed into place, and the trench reversed—minutes of mad excitement and insane activity. We were without consciousness of danger, hypnotized by the work to be done.

We expected a counter-attack, but the German machine-gun we had put at the entrance to the communication trench defended it too well for a Boche to be able to venture in that direction. Toward the trench opposite all the soldiers had their loopholes and were on the watch ready to fire.

We waited. There were false alarms. A man who is a little nervous begins to fire rapidly, his neighbour follows his example, then the squad, then the section, then the whole company

New uniform of Zouave officer,
1915

gets on the rampage. The machine-guns begin to clatter, the second-line troops take alarm, the artillery steps in with a few shells and—the Boches over opposite, bewildered by the hubbub, send up into the sky large interrogation points in the shape of trench rockets, whose rays illumine the grass growing green in the spring, the tangle of wire and several poor dead bodies lying with hands outstretched toward the opposite trench, as if pointing the path of duty to the ones behind.

The counter-attack did not come, but shells upon shells were rained upon us. I gave my canteen of wine to my prisoners, for, after all, they were somewhat to be thanked for our success. It is nothing at all, fifty metres of trench, and yet, it is a few feet of France won back again.

I received my reward; two packages and five letters. In one of the packages was a big April Fool's day fish made of chocolate, all stuffed with candy. I divided the candy among my men, by way of thanks for their splendid conduct, and then I feasted on the letters. Oh, the comfort of letters and words of affection that come to find us out in the midst of our barbarous days!

March 29. Hill 181, in reserve. Shelters deep underground. From the northern crest of this hill can be seen the whole system of trenches, both French and German, in the basin of Perthes. I posted myself with my field-glass between two clumps of bushes: a maze of white lines, much twisted and tangled; from time to time rise blackish clouds. The ruins of Perthes become every day more mournful. I was driven from my post by shells.

Every hour, exactly and methodically, two batteries fire their twelve shells. Forewarned, forearmed. When the moment is past, there is nothing more to fear for one hour. Unfortunately, one of the lieutenants was killed by a shell that was so very unmindful of usage as to seek him in his dug-out.

I had the honour this morning to be shaved under fire. The barber of the company was busy relieving me of a two days' growth of beard when shells began to fall not far from us. "Go on," I cried; and though my barber's hand shook, he cut off neither my nose nor my ears.

I have discovered a stove with some stovepipe. The infirmary didn't want it, and simply threw it away. I had it set up in my dugout where the air is decidedly chilly. With the pine boughs from the woods, roundabout, which my orderly stuffs in, it keeps me warm and enables me to make some good chocolate.

It is cold. Tonight, we shall have to go to the first line to take planks and wire. But what a good cup of tea I shall have when I come back!

March 30. Last night a blizzard came down upon us. It was doubtless due to the violent displacement of air caused by the terrible bombardment that never for a moment ceases.

I came in late—about three o'clock. We had to do a lot of trotting about; the communication trenches took up the snow and were beginning to be muddy again. Oh, this abominable Champagne mud!

Today we were bombarded even more than usual. Several men imprudently went to walk in full view of the enemy. Naturally shells came after them, so now the men are forbidden to go out of the shelters.

I slept all the morning in front of my snoring little stove. Played cards this evening. I feel as if I were rapidly sinking to the level of the brute. For variety we go to the trenches tonight.

March 31. Our last days in Champagne. It seems we are to be laid off to recuperate and will change sectors afterward. One would say that before we go the authorities want us to become profoundly familiar with the landscape of this desolate region. We are in the second line, and in front of us stretches the panorama of all the trenches we have held, beginning with Hill 181. The weather is clear. The snow did not last. We can see the woods, stripped bare by shells, as well as the whole labyrinth of trenches and communications, then the ruins of the stricken village of Perthes. With my glass I can make out the first trench I occupied. I recognise it from certain little details, but we have gone a long way ahead since then, more than a kilometre.

Day comparatively calm. Nothing to do except be ready to sustain a possible attack. We sleep, read, or play cards.

The Boches are still bombarding Perthes and Hill 181. The

big *marmites* send up into the night splendid luminous volcanoes, or else burst above the trenches in clouds that whirl off down the wind. The curious thing is that you see the explosion long before you hear it, and the hiss of the bomb sounds directly overhead at the very moment when it is bursting in the distance. I had to explain this phenomenon to my men, whose knowledge of acoustics is not very extensive.

I have just witnessed a magnificent and terrible sight—a German attack in close formation crushed in less time than it takes to tell it. To the east, in the direction of Beausejour, was an intense bombardment; then through my glass I could see grey masses emerge, gesticulating and densely crowded together. This attack was caught between two curtains of fire. The raging 75's hurled a curtain of fire in front of them, keeping them from advancing, and one behind them that made it impossible for them to get back to their trenches.

They were wiped out to the very last man. There was a mad dance in the air of scattered limbs, mingled with clouds of dirt and smoke. The incredible part of it is that nothing was left on the ground, or next to nothing. It was as if the bodies of those men had been volatilised and made one with the air. We were transfixed with horror and filled with rapturous hope. May the fight in the open be not delayed! Our 75's will quickly give us the victory.

Holy Thursday. Our aviators are floating gracefully about in the twilight—a twilight divinely calm. It is Holy Week. The strains of the great Johann Sebastian and of "*Parsifal*" keep running through my head.

Orders have come. We are to be relieved this evening. We are going to recuperate and then, they say, to Alsace. I shall be so happy to have a chance to fight on the soil we have won back.

This is our last day in Champagne. I am leaving without regret this land of desolation where I have known difficult hours and a few splendid moments. What tried me most sorely was this mole-like existence, I who am always longing for large action and open and intense fighting with an enemy who is before your eyes.

The Boches have been bombarding rather violently. That is to be expected since it is Holy Thursday. But in spite of everything, there has been something religious in the calm of the elements these latter days. Nature is at her devotions. This evening is superb. Shells are bursting in great numbers, and the little church of Perthes totters as if it were about to fall. Through the loopholes comes the mew of spent bullets, but these noises disturb but little the heavenly serenity of the twilight.

Larks are singing, full-throated, a sublime paean of life and joy. In the distance lie the dead, and the frightful, mangled corpse of the village of Perthes.

CHAPTER 8

A Month Away from the Trenches

(For a month our life is spent in marches and more or less prolonged stays in various encampments in the region of the Meuse—a calm existence, without many events of interest. My journal relates only a few scattered incidents.)

April 3. First stage. Left *Cabane-Puits* this morning at three, and reached here at eight.

Little village partly destroyed by the Boches, barbarously, when they were obliged to fall back at the time of the Battle of the Marne. I am billeted in the house of a peasant woman who has told us many tales of their atrocities. The church is in ruins. It seems they locked up in it a very old grandmother and then set fire to it. A striking thing in the midst of the ruins of this church is a statue, still standing—the only one—a statue of Joan of Arc made of plaster, her sword broken, her face blackened with smoke, her banner half gone, but proud and erect, truly a stirring sight.

What a fine subject for an article for Maurice Barres! That virgin symbolising our will to conquer, France wounded and bleeding, but still valiant and undaunted and full of faith. I am told the statue of Joan of Arc at the entrance to the Cathedral of Rheims has not been touched by shells either. It is as if the soul of our country, incarnated in our superb heroine, wished to manifest itself thus to its defenders.

There is a rumour that we shall go to the Dardanelles. What luck that would be! Perhaps I could rejoin my brother who enlisted at eighteen and has just started with the Expeditionary Force.

April 6. We have been on the march for three days. I cannot quite make out the reason for all this marching. Certainly, we are not on the way to fight, for then we should go by rail. It isn't rest, either, thirty kilometres a day of rather hard marching. And then we march in broad daylight. Perhaps it is to throw the enemy off the scent and simulate extensive shifting of troops.

We have crossed the rich pasture lands of the Argonne and the deep, thick forests to the north of which the fighting is in progress. The sight of all this wonderful vegetation has suddenly made me realise that spring is here. The desolation of Champagne—a real desert, with a few clumps of mutilated pines—had given scarcely a hint of its coming. Here there are perfumes and flowers, gayety, pleasant sunshine, birds.

But not everything is gay. We have come through many a wrecked and desecrated village—one especially in which not a single house was left standing. It happened that a sort of wooden shed just outside the village hid the ruins. The band was marching with our battalion that day. The band-master, as usual, had them play a march, and we prepared to file into the village at attention. Then, in our proudest trim, with clarions and flourish of trumpets, we entered suddenly upon a blackened, blasted street between two long heaps of rubbish—not a house, not a living soul, only chaos and emptiness. A strange contrast—that sparkling music with those ruins. But was not this also an act of faith—a promise?

As a rule, we set out about eight in the morning and at one o'clock make a long halt. A rolling kitchen for each company has been included in our regimental train since our departure from the trenches. When we arrive, generally rather tired, we have hot coffee and soup. In the evening on reaching encampment we salute the flag and everyone gets settled in his quarters. Villages in ruins for the most part. There has been no fighting here, but, when they left, the Germans set fire to things everywhere.

At B.-sur-A. is a marvellous Gothic church in the purest style very nearly wrecked. Oh, destroyers of cathedrals! It brings

French soldiers in the Argonne Forest

freshly to my mind the great grief I felt on learning of the burning of Notre Dame de Rheims. Since that moment I have sworn hatred to the Germans. To kill men is, after all, the business of war and it can be explained, even if it cannot be excused. But to try to kill the soul of a whole epoch, the sublime and imposing spirit of the Middle Ages, which had put into its cathedrals all its faith, all its aspirations, all its life!—

The Germans are jealous of the splendour of our country, and they who have raised their Gothic monuments only in the school of France—for Gothic was born in the Île de France— they who have had the wit only to imitate are determined to be first and foremost in the art of destruction. And they know very well that the French will not make reprisals and that Nuremberg and the Wartburg will still be standing after our victory.

April 9. On the banks of the Meuse between Verdun and Saint-Mihiel.

The taking of Éparges has just been announced to us. It is a great success, and great in consequences, I think. We have been brought here as an army of reinforcements to be used in case of need. But our comrades took the mountain without us.

We rest, we exercise mildly. I have been boating a little on the Meuse. At night I like to climb the heights above the village, where one can see the searchlights of Verdun sweeping the sky.

I play a while at the church every day. The band of our regiment gives a daily concert at four.

Much bustle and stir. Endless convoys pass; Boche 'planes come along from time to time and are driven off by our artillery.

April 14. We are kept continually on the move. Now we are headed south.

A splendid ceremony yesterday—the decoration of our flag. Our regiment received the *Croix d'Honneur* for its conduct in Champagne.

The whole army corps was massed in a vast area of untilled fields. Bluecoats everywhere. It was very beautiful. The generals arrived and passed along our front, while we all presented arms. Then the flags of all the regiments were placed side by side, with their escort of honour. Three of the number were to be decorated, and were set a little in advance of this splendid group of shimmering rags floating triumphantly in the wind. All the bands together played the *Marseillaise*. I could not see much, I was so far away, but I did see the general kiss the flags which seemed to droop toward him, and I clearly heard the swelling notes of our national hymn flung to the sky by the bands and by our hearts. Then the whole army corps, bayonets and sabres bared, defiled.

With our beloved standard we returned to cantonment. The colonel made us march before it once more. The glory of our flag was reflected on each one of us and we were very proud.

April 20. Continual marches. Springtime. Rest.

Very uniform life. On reaching a village, after lodging my men, I always sally forth to find the church and play the organ. It is my great joy.

The other day we had execution parade. Two soldiers of the regiment were court-martialled for refusing to go to the trenches and hiding while the others were fighting. They were condemned to hard labour.

In the morning the regiment assembled in a hollow square. Three battalions formed three sides; the fourth was made up of the machine-gun corps, the sanitary corps, and the band. On the arrival of the condemned men, who were dressed in the chestnut brown costume of the convict, their heads shaved, without the slightest vestige of anything military, the colonel ordered us to fix bayonets and shoulder arms.

The prisoners were brought into the middle of the square under the conduct of four soldiers with fixed bayonets. The drums beat a ruffle—a long, low roll followed by complete silence. Then a sergeant-major read the sentence. The drums rolled once more, after which the two men passed along in front of the ranks—supreme ignominy for those who are unworthy to bear arms. Then they were handed over to the *gendarmes* and we all dispersed.

April 22. Reached the banks of the Marne-Rhine Canal,

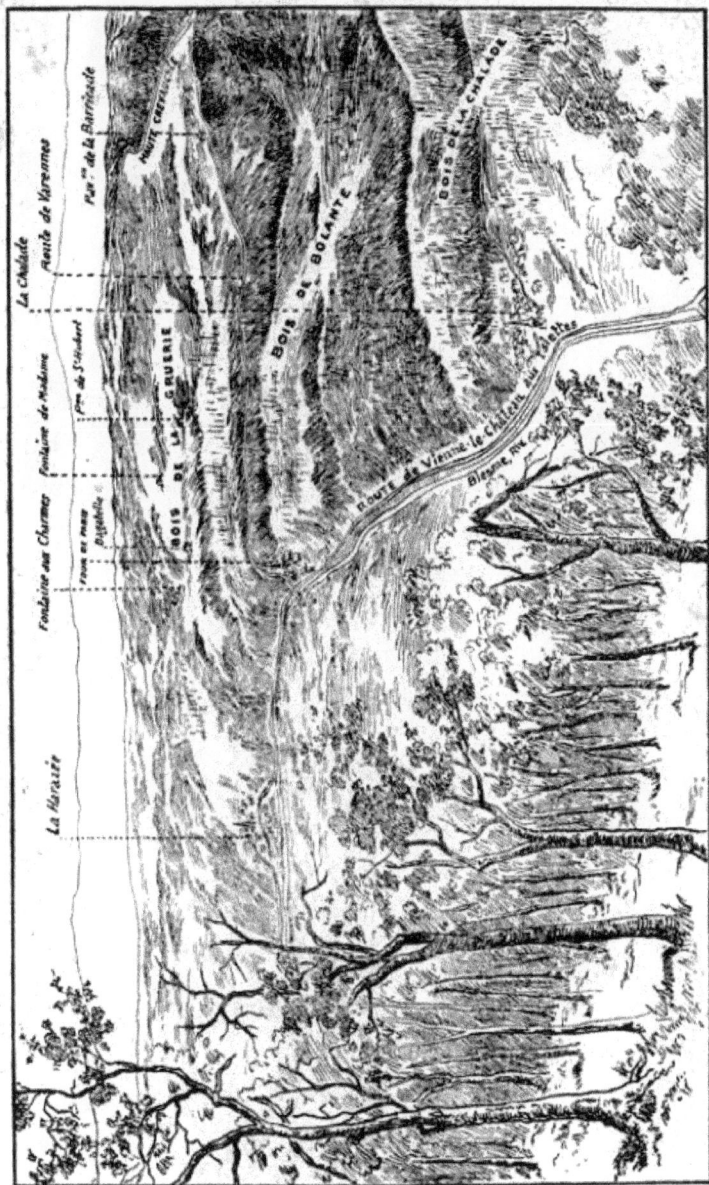

PANORAMIC VIEW OF THE ARGONNE FOREST

along which I have had so many beautiful walks near Nancy in the old days. We are going to entrain. For what point? For Alsace, perhaps, or the Dardanelles.

April 25. Neither Alsace nor the Dardanelles. The secret was well kept. We did not know where we were going until we actually arrived. To the Somme, not far from Amiens.

Our journey was a long one. Leaving Bar-le-Duc at 3 a.m. we did not get out of the train until 11 at night. It was a bitter disappointment when I found I was turning my back on Alsace. I began to follow on my map the branch lines leading toward the south. There were two. We passed them by. We were going in the direction of Paris. We followed the battlefield of the Marne—Cézanne, Terte-Gauche, La Fère-Champenoise, Coulommiers. Along the railroad tracks were trenches, and individual shelters, shell holes, and graves—graves everywhere, either big, common graves decorated with flowers and inscriptions, many-coloured, or else separate graves. But over them all waves the bright tricolour, joyously. They lie in the midst of a veritable flower garden of flags, those who have died for our country.

We met an armoured train run by marine fusiliers. The big guns are graced by the names of women: La Joconde, Josephine, etc. The marines made friendly signals to us as we passed.

And then, toward evening, we reached the outskirts of Paris, in all the adorable beauty of springtime and blossoming trees, to say nothing of its houses, real ones, big, beautiful, luxurious. We had come so near forgetting what they looked like. And the women smiled, and waved to the soldiers who were going off to defend them.

Very near Paris we stopped for two hours, so near that half an hour in an omnibus would have brought us out at the Opéra. We stayed there a long time, with our eyes fixed upon the Capital, and many of us were sad at being so close to those who were dear to us when they so little suspected it. The bugle for departure brought me back from my reveries, and we plunged once more into the night.

At 11 o'clock we detrained and marched until about 2 a.m. Before daybreak we were under shelter. Orders had arrived. We were forbidden to go out in the daytime except when it was possible to keep out of sight. It was essential for the enemy to remain in ignorance of our presence. A very strict watch was instituted against enemy aviators. Patrols provided with field-glasses were stationed on the heights; beside each patrol was a bugler.

As soon as an aeroplane was sighted, long, slow bugle notes indicated that everyone must hide. *Staccato* notes meant that the danger was over. There were numerous alarms—Boche 'planes going to throw bombs on Amiens, also several French 'planes. By way of precaution, the bugle is sounded for every kind of air-craft and the short notes indicating "danger past" re-echo as soon as the sentry spies on the wings of the 'plane the tricolour cockade.

I am billeted at the house of a cheery and charming peasant woman who is kindness itself. She dotes on officers and treats us royally. I wish it might last, this life of peace and comfort. But something is brewing. The storm will burst before long. Of that much I am certain.

April 27. Delicious *far niente*. I am enthroned in idleness like a *pasha*. We are not allowed to show ourselves, so our rest is absolute. But we are well taken care of, and I am not complaining. Meanwhile the commander calls us together each day to expound the principles of the new tactics. There are not to be any more little local attacks, like those in Champagne, but big attacks, and the unit of combat will be the company and no longer the section.

The goal we must aim at is to take at a single blow all the enemy's trenches, so as to push him back into the open. First, the artillery will hammer the Boche trenches; then we shall have to jump over them, while crews of "trench-cleaners" follow in our wake to put in order the trenches thus conquered. The men of the crews are armed with revolvers and knives.

Decidedly the war is daily growing more terrible.

There are other principles, too, that have reference to working in concert with the artillery. But I think it is lunch time.

April 30. We start this evening. There is to be a grand offensive. Some great stroke is being prepared. Will it be the decisive one? I still dream the same dream that haunted me in the training-camp; the grand entry into Berlin, Unter den Linden, but especially the triumphal return to Paris, under the Arc de l'Étoile, down the Champs-Elysées.

I am rather sorry to leave the life of comfort and good cheer I have been leading these days. But thanks to this respite I shall be all the more ready for work, I think.

It is a month since I left Champagne. For a month we have been going about from village to village, from Champagne to the Meuse, from the Meuse to Lorraine, from Lorraine to Flanders. I have seen many countrysides. I have lodged in many villages. Everywhere we have had a marvellous reception, of a kind to make us forget the hardships that are past, and grow strong for those to come.

CHAPTER 9

Before the Grand Offensive (Artois, May 1-8, 1915)

May 1. Here we are near Arras, on the eve of returning to the trenches.

We have had a long journey, in order to travel a very few miles; we left at night, of course, and arrived late at night at Saint-Pol. On coming out of the station we found before us a long train of autobuses waiting to transport us to the front. They were big goods trucks, very powerful, arranged with four seats each, on which there was room for twenty men. Then the companies were divided by turns into groups of twenty, and the men took their places. The officers had a very comfortable motorcar. It did not take more than half an hour to get everybody settled; the swiftness was marvellous. Then this train that bore nearly a thousand men set out into the darkness. Not a light was lighted. Every effort was made to maintain secrecy.

For two solid hours we jolted along at a lively clip over roads that were torn to pieces by the countless convoys which pass every minute of the day and night. We were literally shrouded in dust when we arrived at daybreak at Agnez-les-Duisans. There we got out, the companies formed once more, and we took a bite of breakfast by the side of the road while the quartermasters went ahead to look after billets. Ours was roomy and well supplied with straw; unfortunately, in the course of the day it was discovered that the straw was full of fleas, and the men had to move out and take refuge in cramped quarters.

Arras 1915

We are forbidden to go out in groups. A vigilance service has been organised as before. We have been watching the manoeuvring of a captive "sausage" balloon, a kind of balloon that is shaped and ballasted in such a way as to prevent its being driven about at the mercy of every wind, like the spherical balloons.

Our mess is well installed. My colleague R. always bestirs himself to find the right place, and he is lucky.

Tomorrow we return to the trenches. There is great massing of troops in this region. So, this is where the great stroke will be delivered.

May 3. Once more we take up the life of war. We have been in the trenches since last night. We had nearly lost the wont of shot and shell, though we are managing to keep up a good face. But how different this is from Champagne! Here it is comfortable, almost to the point of luxury, and the sector is as calm as calm—a few isolated cannon shots now and then just to let each other know we are here.

Two of the four sections of my company are in the first line; the two others are in the support trenches. Between the two groups is the captain in a strongly sheltered dug-out, with the telephone nearby. In front of the trench are two listening-posts, where two men and a corporal are continually on the watch, protected by a net from the enemy's grenades. I am in a trench about eighty metres from the German lines. This trench is admirably arranged.

A bench dug in the wall serves at once as a seat and as a place to fire from; the soldier who is about to fire mounts on it and fires through an improved loophole—large on the inside and smaller toward the enemy, so that the Boches cannot easily get a line on the person who is firing. The trench is about eight feet deep and in the sides have been hollowed out roomy individual shelters, a sort of niche with plenty of room for one man.

There are two mines sunk between us and the enemy. I intend to go and see them. My dug-out has two storeys, a bedroom containing a couch of earth covered with straw, and some planks for shelves; underneath, at a depth of eight or ten metres, is a dug-out containing cartridges and grenades. The main store

93

of munitions is near the captain.

The men, too, are comfortably installed. Each one has his own hole which he can make bigger or arrange to suit himself. Besides, in case of a heavy bombardment, it is possible to take refuge in the big mine galleries. Finally, two machine-guns, carefully protected, guard the space that separates us from the Boches.

And then, there are casks of water in the trench itself. Could anything be more unlike the trench at Perthes? The fatigues fill them daily from the well not far distant, and we can drink as much as we please. In order to keep the water cool, the casks are put deep in the ground. There are a number of round-bottomed metal bowls in the trench, the use of which was explained to us in the daily bulletin. On account of the great number of head wounds, it has been found advisable to adopt helmets in the French Army.

Meanwhile, these little bowls can be put inside the cap to protect the head. I tried one and found it heavy. But I shall certainly use it if there is any need. Our ingenious *poilus* discover all sorts of uses for these bowls. They empty their pockets into them, put into them the supply of cartridges that every man is obliged to have by him at his loophole, thus keeping the cartridges free of the mud which clogs and spoils the guns. And I used one for a wash-basin, and helped myself to a little of the drinking-water to wash in.

Although the sector was quiet, I did not sleep. The orders were that one man out of two was to be allowed to sleep. The arrangement of the trench did not permit taking one half-section for a certain time and then the other. That would have required awkward shifting about, so I hit upon another plan. I paired off the men according to the old principle of putting chums to work together. Either one or the other was to be always awake. They were allowed to arrange the details to suit themselves. Sometimes the one who was least tired good-naturedly kept watch and let the other sleep as long as he wished.

I like to leave a certain amount of liberty and initiative to my men. It always pleases them, and the service is much better attended to. During the night we keep up a good deal of firing. This bothers the German workers or their listening-patrols and prevents our men from getting drowsy.

I went to the listening-post, about sixty metres from the German trenches. It is hazardous to look out except with a periscope. The landscape is very nearly as monotonous as in Champagne: barbed wire, grey lines, and a few dead bodies lying between the lines, but the vegetation is richer and more luxuriant. In front of the listening-post is a mine. In case of attack the earth can be blown up twenty metres in advance, simply by lighting a bickford fuse.

So, the sector is perfectly clean, comfortable, and quiet. Very little work is done except at night, and even then, not much.

At noon we are going into the support trench.

Evening. In the second line. We are in deep dug-outs, well-protected, regular cellars, abundantly provided with straw. I have been sleeping a little. Our food is brought to us at the captain's. A warming apparatus makes it possible for us to have excellent hot meals. The men are well treated, too. The kitchens are much easier of access than in Champagne.

We have been warned by telephone to be on the lookout for a probable German attack. It seems they have been throwing to the English numerous proclamations, all ending with:—

"When is that French attack coming?"

So, they are expecting to be attacked, and perhaps they will forestall our offensive. In case of an alarm I am to betake myself with my men to the first line. Our position, of course, is settled in advance. At five o'clock there was a sort of commotion, a false alarm, cooked up by the enemy, doubtless, and we all hurried to our fighting posts in the first line, and then—marched back again.

Tonight, we shall have to keep our eyes and ears open, and all the officers are to take turns in going the rounds. My hours are nine and two.

May 4. Two more false alarms last night. A soldier thinks he hears suspicious noises, gets excited, and fires like mad. The panic goes churning down the line and raises a regular hurricane in its trail.

In making the rounds, I went over the whole ground occupied by the company. From time to time a flash from my electric lamp showed me the way through the deserted communication trenches. Everyone was at his post. The enemy could come on if he wished. To tell the truth, not a single shell was sent our way. The Boches had never been less troublesome.

Today it is raining, and I regret to see that the soil of Artois gets muddy easily too. Having nothing else to do, I asked an officer of the engineering corps for permission to go into the mine. He consented most willingly, and went down with me into the gallery. It is solidly built, and supported by heavy planks, for the brittle earth might easily stop up this narrow space. I had to crawl on all fours a long time before reaching the end, where the listening-post was. Two men were on duty there, standing with their ears close to the wall, in the yellowish light of a single candle. We were under the German trench.

On listening carefully, I made out a faint murmur of voices, very indistinct and muffled. I should not have objected to overhearing the conversation of those men who were in all likelihood to die before many days were spent. The large explosion chamber of the mine was to be stuffed with cheddite, and at the given moment, an electric spark would send that trench and its inhabitants on a journey in the air. It wasn't at all pleasant down in that hole. The air was stifling, and I was glad enough, after another long crawl, to find myself in the open again, if the trench maybe called the open.

In order to guard against gas bombs, we have been given horrible, nightmarish masks, goggles set in a kind of pig jowl or snout made of rubber and containing a solution of ammonia. They make you look like a wild animal, and as soon as I got mine, I put it on for the benefit of my *poilus*. They nearly laughed themselves into fits.

But life in general is calm, too calm even. I am reading *Anna Karenina*, that came by mail yesterday, and smoking endless pipes. The men make lots of aluminium rings. As soon as a shell lands they start out to look for the fuse, of which they fashion very artistic little rings. My soldiers have given me several. I am on

FRENCH INFANTRY ATTACKING A GERMAN TRENCH
IN THE ARTOIS OFFENSIVE

most friendly terms with them all. At odd times I have bought them little extras in the way of wine or sweets, and then I manage things so that they get their letters before any of the other sections. The letters come toward midnight, with the fatigue who brings rations.

I am always on hand, and along with my own correspondence I take that of my men. It is the one great joy of the day, so why should it be deferred? To be sure, it is because I am so keen on letters myself that I like the men to share my pleasure. And if they have no light, they have permission to come to my dug-out, which is always lighted. They insist on my taking some of all their good things, candies, cigarettes, or what-not, when a package comes. But I can find a way to even things up.

I think I have my men well in hand. I shall be able to do some good work with them when the time comes.

May 5. At noon, returned to the first line. After that the day was eventful. It was decided, by way of preparation for future offensives, to furnish the attacking sections with red and white pennons, which were to serve as signals to the artillery, and mark the first French lines. By this means the artillery will not risk peppering its compatriots in the course of an advance. Today the order came to raise the pennons over our first lines, so that our artillery can get the range of the enemy's positions. At two o'clock, therefore, they were hoisted.

The astonishment of the Boches was promptly made manifest by a whirlwind of bullets which converted these common bits of cloth into glorious trophies. Then our artillery turned loose. It was our duty to observe the range and rectify it by telephone. One by one, with mathematical precision, big shells lighted on the German positions. There must be a formidable number of batteries, for without a moment's pause or cessation shells poured on the Boche trench for three full hours.

Meanwhile, very naturally, our friends across the way began to get peevish and sent off a few blasts of little 77's, which afforded great satisfaction to the makers of rings. One could hear them coming very distinctly; first, the six reports of the battery, then a hiss, then a detonation, not very terrifying. I was in the middle of the trench with my eye glued to a periscope. Several shells landed near; one fell on a decaying corpse in the midst of the wire, spreading about for several minutes the horrible heavy odour that reminded me of the night we buried the dead in Champagne. Another stupid shell chose to fall in the passage that led to my dug-out. The bags of sand were tumbled all about and it took more than half an hour's work before I could get into my quarters. My things were not at all damaged.

And yet, at one moment explosive shells rained thick and fast, two or three on the parapet, blowing to bits several loopholes. The machine-gunners, who were playing cards near their gun, shut their dug-out with a tent-sheet. It is a thing I have often noticed and proves that, after all, man is not so different from the ostrich. One has the illusion of being secure behind the most flimsy barrier, if only it keeps out the sight of the danger—a hedge, a plank, a tent-sheet. It is an insult to reason, but that doesn't matter. Brute instinct knows no reason.

So, the sector that on our arrival seemed asleep has had a rude awakening. Everything points to a coming offensive. I certainly hope we shall have a share in it.

May 6. Night calm. The Boches seemed non-existent. Our artillery quieted down. I was wakeful notwithstanding. The responsibility is too great.

It is raining hard. There is water in the bottom of the trench, and it is impossible to move without taking a disagreeable foot-bath.

But the aviators give signs of great activity. Since morning we have had the joy of watching several reconnaissances. The 'planes were hotly bombarded, but to no purpose.

Their flight must have been successful, for no sooner had they returned than our artillery set up a terrible spitting at the German trenches. It was not hurried, but was a slow, continuous, methodical fire which must have been very deadly. From the second line we sent off the Little winged bombs, the "cauliflowers" whose acquaintance we made in Champagne. They leap up, not very high, then hesitate an instant before they swoop down upon the Boches, exploding with a muffled thud which makes the ground tremble clear to our trench, while a spout of black smoke rises and floats a long time. In all the sectors where I have been, the superiority of our artillery becomes every day more evident.

After dinner the question was telephoned:

What are the special points the different section commanders would like to see battered by the artillery in case of a drive?

I asked for the collaboration of all my men. I had the corporals explain to them the signs by which they could recognise the machine-gun positions: better defences, loopholes bigger, bags of sand more numerous and more carefully arranged. I took my glass and observed minutely all the points of the German trench. I went to the listening-post, and with the help of a much-perfected field-glass periscope, which magnifies in addition to giving a view over the edge, I probed the German position.

At the end of more than an hour's work, utilising the observations of my men, I was able to fix almost to a certainty the positions of four machine-guns. I marked on the plan of the trenches that had been given us the exact points to be hammered, and the document was sent along the hierarchical paths and in due time reached the artillery.

Then we indulged in a little distraction. As the rain had stopped, I went to two of my best marksmen and proposed a match. It is very amusing to try one's skill in shooting. The objective point is a Boche loophole, that is to say, a piece of steel plate. If the balls touch, one hears a metallic ring and the hum of the ricochet. I made a good score, but I placed only nine balls out of ten, and was beaten by P. who got in all ten. The prize was a package of cigarettes.

Everybody is in a good humour today. There is a great buzz of conversation. Some of the men are playing checkers, others cards. One man who is the happy recipient of an accordion is favouring us with popular tunes which everybody catches up in chorus. Really, it is very festive.

This evening we go to the second line, in the shelters. Three of the four companies of our battalion are on the firing line, the fourth is in reserve. It is our turn now to be in reserve.

May 7. We are in marvellous shelters, where we laugh defiance to missiles of all sorts and kinds, even the 420's. Behind the second lines, galleries have been sunk, to which broad staircases give access. Around them is a sort of ditch which serves as a yard, on which the entrances open. They are vast tunnels, fifty feet underground, made by the engineers—broad, supported by huge beams, and furnished with plank floors. They are about a hundred feet long, ten feet broad, and ten feet high, and are in every way comfortable. There are beds of straw, bags for pillows and candles for light. In the yard are supplies: grenades, wire, trench shells, and casks of water.

We officers have a special gallery with two compartments, a living-room and a sleeping-room. The living-room is provided with a huge fireplace, a big table, several stools, and a superb lamp. The bedroom is less sumptuous—a large space covered with a thick bed of straw where we shall sleep soundly.

There has been unusual activity along the front these two days. Staff officers keep coming and going. Men have been carrying to the first lines quantities of hand grenades, wire, and ladders. Aeroplanes are circling busily through the air. The artillery sounds like an orchestra tuning its instruments before the symphony. Important events are afoot.

Evening. It's coming! The grand offensive is to be launched over a wide area. In the whole of Flanders, the attempt is to be made to pierce the Boche front. We are going to try to get out of these accursed trenches and fight superbly, face to face.

About five o'clock, just as we were sitting down at table, I was called to the commandant. My colleagues had also been summoned and we received our orders. Tomorrow, at an hour not yet indicated, the regiment is to attack, in concert with those of the nine army corps that are massed in this region. It is the grand offensive—victory, perhaps. We are to go forward and jump over four enemy trenches, previously battered by the artillery, not stopping until we reach a ravine that can be seen through the

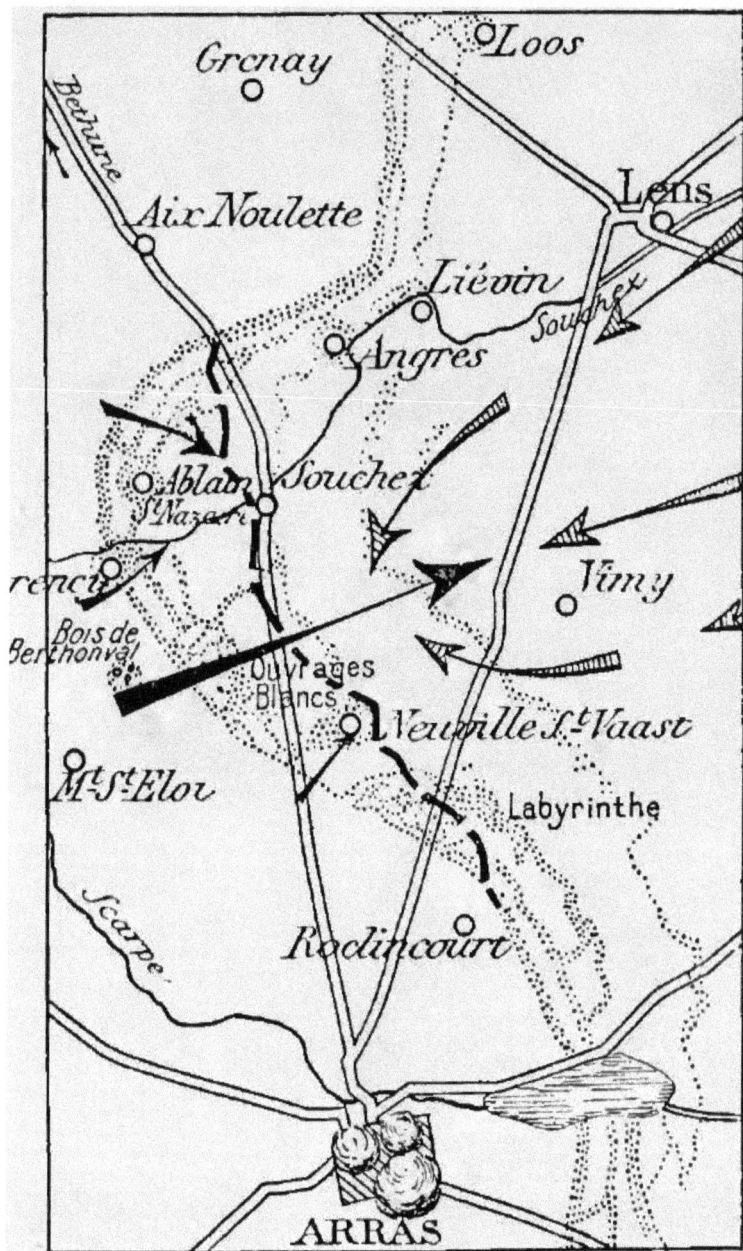

glass eight hundred metres from our first line. We pore over the maps, and make sure of our exact goal. My company is to march at the head in open formation and lead the drive. The commandant thereupon shook hands with each of us in turn, and told us that he counted on every man to do his duty.

I went back to my soldiers to issue the command to get ready. Each man was to have two hundred cartridges, six grenades, and three days' rations, and was to carry his blanket slung crosswise over his shoulder. But while I was consulting with my colleagues the plan of the German positions, a message came that all orders were cancelled. The sudden let-down was not entirely pleasant, but we all shared somewhat the feeling of the sorry jester who said: "All right, that gives us one more day to live."

We count on coming out alive. But the nearness of danger is not without its anguish.

We have been having a fine game of poker. I lost, so I shall be lucky.

I am tired. My fellow officers have been asleep this long time. I am going to imitate them. The boom of our big guns is heavy and deep.

May 8. 10 p.m. It is for tonight. We are to take positions in the first line at 3 a.m. The time of the attack is not yet fixed. I have written a great many letters. Perhaps I have given way to my feelings in some of them. I did not tell my mother. I wrote her that new movements of troops are predicted for the near future, and that she is not to worry if she has no news of me for a while. But I told the truth to my little godmother and to my old friend . . . .

But sadness and farewells I have put behind me. Now I am all a soldier, and a soldier filled with the determination to fight and to conquer, and exalted by the work that is before him. If I die, and these are the last words I am destined to write, I want them to be

Vive—Vive la France.

CHAPTER 10

The Attack

June 9. In the silence and quiet of a little hospital room, near a window where pink and white thorn-trees make a fragrant screen, I am going to recall the nightmare of a month ago, and finish the record of my first campaign.

As I read over the last few pages, the enthusiasm I felt when they were written comes surging back. Neither time nor suffering can take it away from me. But the horror of the hours that followed our offensive on the terrible ninth of May is very nearly a thing of the past. It has been lifted and smoothed away in this peaceful white hospital by the angels who dwell in it— the sublime women of the French Red Cross. Not that I have forgotten any part of the events of that day. The account I shall give of them will be exact.

On the night before the attack, then, we were awakened about midnight by the beginning of the bombardment. Unable to sleep, we arose and got ready ahead of time. At last came the order to go forward to our fighting posts. One by one we moved along the dark, narrow trenches leading to the first lines. Above our head was the constant hissing of our big shells on their way to the Boches. Once in the first line, we spent the long hours of waiting as comfortably as we could.

Dawn came slowly. Through our loop-holes we could discern the grey line of the trenches we were to take, ploughed up by our artillery volcanoes. Regularly, almost mathematically, our heavy shells dropped on the enemy, demolishing their dug-outs, smashing their wire entanglements, shattering their trenches. At times, through my field-glass, I could distinctly see human limbs scattered in the air along with the earth of the explosions.

Meanwhile coffee was brought, and it was welcome in the chill of early morning. I went to each of my men in turn and spoke of that which was nearest his heart. I knew them well, my *poilus*. I tried to make them feel the confidence I felt, and in doing so, my own faith grew stronger and the last faint doubt that oppressed me was driven from my mind.

The bombardment kept growing in intensity. It was seven o'clock. Several artillery officers came into my trench to control the precision of the fire, which was to clear our way of all outside obstacles—wire entanglements, *chevaux-de-frise,* the enemy trenches. The observation post was at a distance from the telephone, and the rectifications given by the officers were repeated down the line from man to man. In a short time, all was regulated and the storm began. It is impossible to realise the din of this firing. Guns of all calibres spit forth their shells with the maximum of rapidity. This lasted three hours, three deafening, maddening hours. In the midst of the storm of steel and fire the brigadier-general arrived. He said a few words to me. I told him I was as sure of my men as of myself. He seemed satisfied and gave me the hour of attack, ten o'clock.

Ten o'clock! Everyone looked at his watch. Nine o'clock. So, in an hour then. It is an hour tense with emotion. Faces that are near give place to other faces. The hand seeks some loved token, the eye lingers on a letter, a photograph, or is fixed upon the *Book of Prayer*. Five minutes to ten! I take my place at the foot of my ladder. In those last moments thoughts come rapidly. On this ladder hangs our destiny. In the trench there is relative security. What will become of us at the top of those four rounds? But no one thinks of hesitating. We seem to be in the grasp of some unknown and mighty force.

I seize my revolver and make sure of my grenades. One minute to ten. At this instant comes a rumbling detonation which causes the ground to tremble as if shaken by an earthquake. Our mines have exploded. This is the time.

"Attention! Forward, *mes petits*, and *Vive la France!*"

This cry burst from every throat, and I sprang up my ladder, followed by my men. From that moment I was carried forward by the intoxication of the assault. I ran, gesticulating and yelling. I did not see, but rather felt, my men close to me, running by my side, and, like myself, drunk with a sublime madness. We reached the first German trench. We threw hand grenades. But no living thing was there. Confusedly in my onward rush I saw heaps of earth and corpses. The bombardment had almost levelled the trench. Forward, still forward. We kept running breathlessly, carried away by the strange fascination of victory and by the joy of treading the soil we were giving back to France. I went ahead, unconscious of those who were falling by the way. My intelligence was numbed. A greater force was urging me on.

After passing the second trench, I noticed that our ranks had thinned, but we went on and plunged into the third trench. A furious hand-to-hand fight followed. I unloaded my revolver almost instinctively on a German who was aiming at me. By this time our second wave of assault was coming up to us. I quickly decided to join it and push forward. I was covered with sweat and blood—with the blood of the Boche I had killed. I was in a frenzy. I ran toward the fourth trench, the last one to be captured before reaching our goal. I went on, hypnotized by that trench which seemed to be running to meet me. I wanted it. It belonged to me. I could see the enemy through the gaps our artillery had made in their defences.

Suddenly I fell. I was alone. Above my head was the constant whizzing of bullets; nearby, the significant snorting of a machine-gun. At first, I was a little stunned, then I attempted to rise and felt that my right arm moved with difficulty. My coat was covered with blood. My arm hung limp. I felt it. I tried to understand. Wounded, of course. But what of my soldiers? I raised my head; a bullet struck the ground very near. I fell back, but I had had time enough to see. Nobody in front of me. Nobody behind me. Corpses all around. I was alone, ten yards from the enemy's trench. I could see the Boches moving in it. With my left hand I got hold of my revolver that was still hanging to the fingers of my other hand. But what was the use of firing

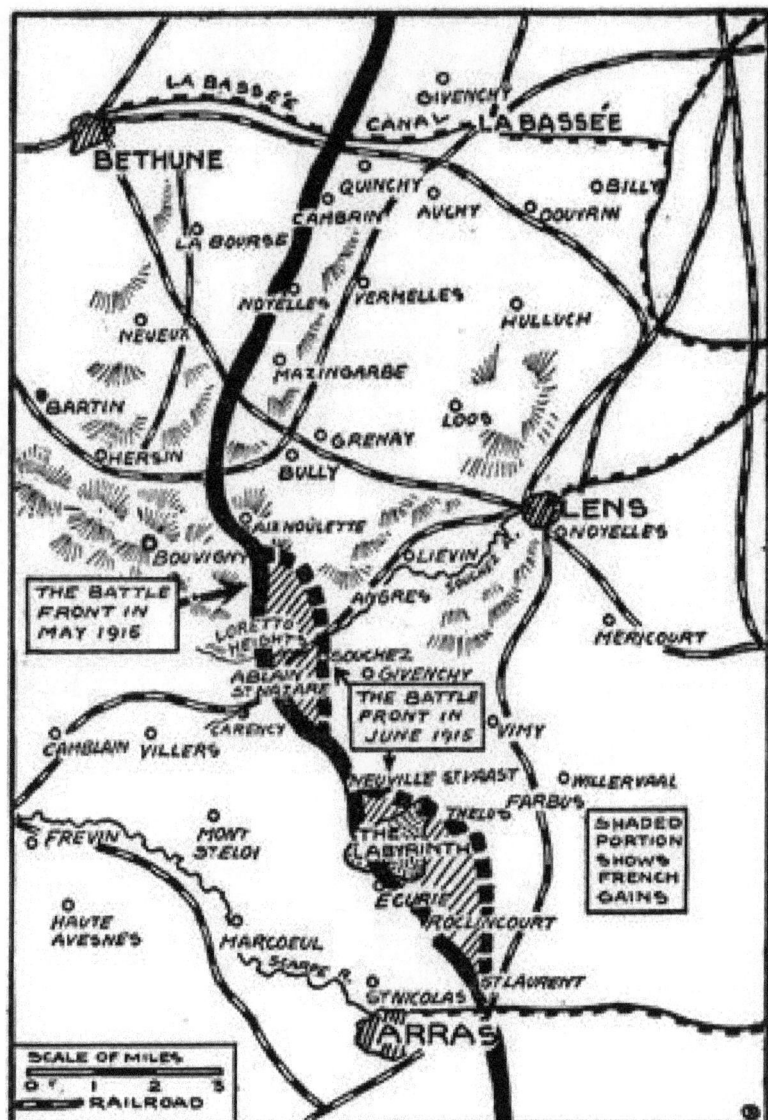

LA BASSÉE CANAL — LA BASSÉE

GIVENCHY

BÉTHUNE

QUINCHY   O BILLY

CAMBRIN   AUCHY   DOUVRIN

LA BOURSE

NOYELLES   VERMELLES   HULLUCH

NEUEUX

MAZINGARBE

BARTIN

CHERSIN   GRENAY   LOOS

BULLY

AIX NOULETTE   LENS   NOYELLES

BOUVIGNY   LIEVIN

THE BATTLE
FRONT IN
MAY 1915

ANGRES

LORETTO
HEIGHTS   SOUCHEZ   MÉRICOURT

ABLAIN
ST NAZAIRE   GIVENCHY   THE BATTLE
FRONT IN
JUNE 1915

CARENCY   VIMY

CAMBLAIN VILLERS   NEUVILLE ST VAAST   WILLERVAAL

FARBUS

FREVIN   MONT
ST ELOI   THELUS

THE
LABYRINTH   SHADED
PORTION
SHOWS
FRENCH
GAINS

HAUTE
AVESNES   ECURIE

MARCOEUL   ROCLINCOURT

Starpe R.

ST NICOLAS   ST LAURENT

ARRAS

SCALE OF MILES
0   1   2   3
RAILROAD

left-handed? I should miss and they would make an end of me.

To advance was impossible. To go back was equally impossible. The least move would be my death. The bullets above my head kept up a fearful hum. It seemed as if I could not possibly get out of this, and passive, resigned, I flattened myself against the ground and remained motionless.

This situation could not last. If I did not get under shelter, one of those bullets would surely find me out. Nearby, within a few yards, a slight rise in the ground indicated a possible cavity. With great care, without apparent motion, inch by inch, I dragged myself to it. Think of my joy. It was a large funnel, dug out by a German mine, and a score of wounded had taken refuge in it. Still another effort and I found myself among them. The cavity was five or six yards deep, and very wide at the top. A few dead lay prone upon the edge, poor fellows, killed at the moment when, like myself, they saw salvation in that hole.

I recognised in the crater three of my own men. One of them, wounded in the thigh, was applying a bandage with the help of a comrade. When this was done, he cut the sleeve of my coat, then my jacket sleeve, and finally my shirt sleeve. He poured a little tincture of iodine on the wound. The elbow was pierced through and through. He dressed it with bandages from the package every soldier carries, and made a sling with a piece of tent-sheet. And then, profoundly moved to find ourselves there after that mad race, officer and man met in a silent embrace, expressing by that gesture what words failed to voice.

The captain of the company which marched immediately behind us was also there, downcast, raging like the rest of us at being in this stupid and terrible situation. Some of the men were slightly wounded, but one man had a big hole in his stomach. The poor wretch lay panting and moaning. At times he screamed in spite of our efforts to keep him still. The cries were heard by the Boches whose trench was scarcely ten yards away, and in accordance with their noble custom of killing the wounded, they threw grenades in our direction. Fortunately, they fell short of us, but they increased our anxiety, as well as our disgust and hatred.

Above our heads the air was lashed with a terrible cross-fire. The sad truth began to come home to me that our advance had been checked after the third trench. And what of my men, my *poilus* whom I so loved? Dead?

Meanwhile our own plight was extremely critical. Our lives hung by a very slender thread. For the present, the unceasing fire of machine-guns prevented our escape. Sooner or later the Germans would launch a counterattack and put an end to us with their hand grenades. And again, if the French pursued the offensive, they would renew the bombardment, and in all probability, we should be struck by our own shells. As for surrendering to the Boches—they were near enough—every man of us would rather starve in that hole. These thoughts and the pain from my wound prostrated me for a moment. I felt myself losing consciousness and I took a few drops from a flask of cordial that happened to be in my bag, and I revived.

Then came a brief lull. Time dragged along slowly, very slowly. Toward noon a fusillade broke forth in the enemy's trench. A ray of hope. Were the French carrying their attack to the fourth line? A man suddenly stumbled into our crater. He was one of my own soldiers. He was without his equipment. He saw me and, weeping and laughing, embraced me. I asked him where he came from and why he had no gun, no bayonet, no grenades. In a distracted voice he told me his story.

After I had been wounded and knocked down, my soldiers kept on running forward and jumped into the fourth German trench. But their ranks had thinned, and they were too few. Some were killed, others disarmed. The latter were told by the Boches after a time: "You are not wanted. Get out of here." My men were bewildered. They could not understand. Again, they were ordered to leave, and finally they leaped out of the trench and began running back to the French position. The brutes then fired upon them from behind. All were killed evidently, with the exception of this soldier, who owed his life to the crater into which he had providentially fallen.

My grief was intense. I had lost all my brave men, and I was powerless to avenge them. To this mental torture was added the suffering from my wound. The hot rays of the sun came directly upon us. Hand grenades fell again into the crater. We crouched close to the ground.

Presently French 75's and 105's began to burst over the German trench. We watched the shells. They were very, very near us. One 75 exploded just above our heads and the impact threw the body of a dead soldier almost on top of me. It was a terrible feeling to be under the fire of our own guns. Another shell burst and blew to pieces that very soldier of mine who had escaped the odious massacre. We quickly threw a tent-sheet over this abomination. We were fully conscious of the horror of our situation. Another explosion cut off the foot of a sergeant, and in spite of his screams I poured a flask of iodine on his wound. Then, for the first time, I gave up all hope. We had made a sacrifice of our lives and motionless, resigned, we sat silently waiting.

But an idea came to me. There were heavy planks in the bottom of the crater, which had been used to prop the explosion chamber of the mine. With much difficulty we moved them together, leaning them against the side of the crater. Under this shelter we all huddled. Several times our wooden structure was violently shaken by explosions, and our wounds were racked at each shock, but more than that we were not hurt. This lasted a long time, an infinitely long time. The hours do not seem to move under such circumstances.

Finally, the captain, the only man in the crater who was not wounded, declared that he was going to the French trench to have the firing stopped. In spite of our protests, for we knew that he would meet death on the way, he went out under the bombardment.

A long time afterward the firing from our side ceased. Could the captain have reached our trenches? And hope revived in us again. We all wanted to leave this inferno at once. But the German machine-guns started in afresh. We must wait for the night.

The sun was getting low. The bombardment ceased and we came out from under the protection of our planks. We stretched out on the ground, which was all furrowed by shells. The wounded were moaning, some had the death rattle. I was exhausted, and somehow, I fell asleep. When I awoke it was already dusk. The hour of deliverance was near. But as soon as night came, rockets flashed from the German trench and a fusillade burst forth. Possibly some of the wounded had tried to return to our lines and were being shot from behind. Our hope grew dim, and we wondered if we should ever get away. We were horrified to think we might have to spend another day in that hole. Better die at once, die in an effort to get back, die with hope in our hearts.

About nine o'clock the man least wounded among us decided to venture forth. His plan was, on reaching the French line, to request that a trench be dug out in our direction so that we could return in safety. We agreed upon a signal to be given by our machine-guns: twice four sharp shots to establish the communication; three times three slow shots would indicate that we must wait until they came for us; three times three rapid shots that we should have to escape by our own means.

Half an hour or more elapsed. Rockets kept flashing in the night and the machine-guns never stopped. We began to fear for the fate of our comrade. Yet at last came the signal—three times three rapid shots. *Come back, come back, come back,* said the French guns. We had to count on ourselves alone. Then we decided to crawl to our lines.

One by one, at long intervals, we left. Only one could not leave, the man wounded in the stomach. "So, you forsake me," he moaned. I spread my blanket over him and promised to send for him. I knew this was impossible, but my deception might help him to die in hope. I also knew the terror of dying there slowly, and alone, all alone. But he was beyond our help.

The German guns were firing violently on the French positions. We did not realise this during the day, as our anguish and pain kept us from studying the battle. It was foolhardy to go forth under the bombardment, but we were really crazed. A single idea, a fixed idea, remained with us—to go back, to go back by all means, or die. For my own part, I was not quite conscious of what I was doing.

I could not crawl on my stomach. I was obliged to lie on my back, and advance head first toward the French trench. The rockets gave me a glimpse of our lines. They were several hundred yards distant. I pushed myself along with my feet as does a man when swimming on his back. As soon as a rocket flashed its light, I remained motionless, feigning death among the dead. And in those few instants of immobility, I could hear my heart beat, and a vague horrible murmur made up of moans and cries of men dying, and of wounded calling for help. I passed by a soldier who was groaning feebly. I recognised him and tried to drag him with me. With great difficulty I managed to pull him a few feet. And then I saw that I was dragging a corpse.

This Calvary lasted long, frightfully long. Several times I bumped my head into dead bodies. Crawling backward I could not see these obstacles. At one moment, I found myself under a corpse. The body was in a kneeling position and leaning forward. I had its face against my face, and its open eyes seemed to stare at me. The magnesium light of a rocket made that face appear still more livid. I worked myself free and went on over that rough, chaotic ground, falling into shell holes, jostling the dead. But my whole being was strained to the one idea—to go back, to reach the French trench to which I was drawing nearer and nearer. I began talking out loud. Without knowing it, I must have talked a good deal. I found myself saying over half-forgotten snatches of Virgil:—

Est in conspectu Tenedos, uotissima fama
Insula, dives opum. . . .

It was indeed "*in conspectu*," that trench, and likewise "*dives opum*"—richer than any Island of the Blest.

Meanwhile German shells kept falling in rapid succession. I was covered with earth several times, and once roughly shaken up. But now the goal was very near. I shouted with all my might: "France, France, I am a lieutenant of the Eleventh Company." I dimly heard voices saying: "This way, this way." I directed myself by those voices. My strength was almost gone. I got entangled in wire defences. My arm hurt unbearably. A shell that fell near stunned me. I felt myself being seized and pulled. I fell into the trench—the French trench. Then I fainted.

Chapter 11

Evacuation

When I regained consciousness, I was in the dug-out of an officer of the machine-gun section. He gave me some brandy, and I revived. Almost immediately afterward came the Boche counter-attack. It was met by the fire from their own machine-guns, and was quickly beaten back. With my left hand I unloaded the six bullets of my revolver into the dark shadows advancing toward us. This much I could do for my soldiers.

But when the danger was over, my nerve suddenly left me, and I was frightened, as frightened as a child in the dark. I was afraid to go alone to the dressing-station, and waited to walk along with the stretcher-bearers. We had to go a long distance. I realised that we had covered a good deal of ground in the morning, and I was filled with hope. Why should not our men do the same thing the next day, and then the next, until we could raise our heads and say: "Ours the victory!"

When the surgeons had dressed my wound, I was placed on a stretcher and lifted into an ambulance. Then began the journey to the rear.

A day and a half later, after a chaotic ride through the darkness, I reached the hospital of the beautiful little town of Arras, where the wounded are collected from the various dressing-stations. I was taken into a vast ward and undressed by two orderlies, who cut away my coat and jacket and put me to bed between clean sheets. In spite of a battery that was booming right beside the hospital, and in spite of the pain in my arm, I went to sleep, utterly worn out.

The next morning, I was helped into my clothes and put almost immediately into an automobile to be taken toward the rear, ever farther and farther from the din of battle, which was still going on. We met a great number of convoys of troops on their way to reinforce the front, infantry transported in heavy trucks, as we had been ten days before, artillery-drawn by caterpillar tractors, and masses of cavalry waiting for the forward dash. Truly, everything seemed ready for pushing far ahead. And I was enraged at being wounded at such a moment, for the thought of our advance was magnificent and inspiring.

The motor came to a stop in a little village of this luxuriant region of Artois. The hospital where we were cared for momentarily was in the schoolhouse. I was given a hypodermic of serum to prevent tetanus. The schoolmistress, who still kept a single room for her classes, learning that I belonged to the University, asked me to go home to lunch with her. She was exquisitely kind and thoughtful, waiting on me, preparing my food and helping me to eat. Then I lay down on her bed. I was at the end of my strength.

Toward evening I was again put into an automobile, and again came a confused ride over torn-up roads. My arm was very painful. I felt my hand swelling and growing heavy and feverish. It was late when we reached the evacuation hospital, where I once more went to bed. I found there one of my companions in misery, an adjutant wounded in the thigh. The next morning very early we were awakened by violent detonations. It was German aeroplanes throwing bombs on the station and the hospital. One of them fell very near the building where we poor wretches were lying. Could the barbarians attack even us?

In that immense hospital ward was every sort of horrible wound. No part of the body had been spared. But what impressed me most was an officer in the bed next to mine, totally disfigured by a shell—a repulsive monster, ignoble, with neither nose nor lips. I saw him plainly when they were dressing his wound. And it hurt me.

At noon I got into an automobile again, this time to go only as far as the station, where the sanitary train was waiting for us.

There were two kinds of coaches, one with comfortable swinging stretchers for wounded who were not able to sit up, and for the rest of us ordinary first and second-class coaches. I was in a first-class compartment with a lieutenant who was ill, a second lieutenant wounded in the hand, and a colonel who had a quantity of little shell splinters in his leg. I happened to be the worst off of any of them, and it was touching the way they all tried to do some little thing to make me comfortable.

The colonel helped me get settled, cut my meat, almost fed me. He was like a father, and it was very affecting to see this old colonel, all covered with medals, waiting upon a little lieutenant who was scarcely out of his teens.

At the big stations, Amiens particularly, they took off the wounded who were suffering most. But in spite of the pain and fever in my arm, I wanted to stay on the train. I kept thinking it was going to take me to the South, to the Riviera, where my family was at that moment.

At nightfall we arrived just outside of Paris, and there the train waited until morning. It was the same station where we had stopped nearly twenty days before, on returning from the Meuse. In the morning the faithful ladies of the Red Cross came with cheerful smiles to bring us cups of hot coffee. Then the train steamed slowly out. We met some Boche prisoners who were also being evacuated. Be it said to the honour of the French wounded, no cry against the barbarians went up from our train; France knows the respect that is due a vanquished enemy.

After that the train sauntered along all day in the direction of the Loire. We stopped at many stations in peaceful, shaded countrysides, and at each of these havens a few of the wounded got out. At every station, young girls came to bring us flowers, fresh eggs, illustrated papers, and likewise their smiles, admiring, a little tender too, and grateful. I was especially touched by the flowers. They brought them by armfuls and loaded us down. We suddenly began to have a glimmering of our lofty estate as wounded. The attentions of those exquisite women made us almost imagine we had done something worthwhile. But this did not lessen the deep gratitude with which we accepted their gifts.

The debt of gratitude that I vowed from that moment to the women of France has been growing daily greater since I have been in this hospital. I reached here late at night. At the station the wounded were divided among the different hospitals of the town and I was assigned to the hospital of *l'Union des Femmes de France*, a private institution, housed in the buildings of the Girls' Normal School. At the entrance, white figures stood out against the dim light. When I went in, I was met by smiling faces, and two of the ladies accompanied me to my room. There they took off my clothes and gave me my first bath in many days, doing all this simply, gently, tenderly, laughing at me a little if I was embarrassed, as can well be imagined.

Could anything be more wonderful than to see the devotion with which these delicately reared women perform all kinds of unpleasant and unwonted tasks? And always with the same cheerfulness, the same gentleness, the same patience, for wounded soldiers are far from being agreeable at times. If there is any virtue in the soldiers of France, a thousand times more worth are its women, whose very presence and smile brings healing. I fell under the charm of it at once, and my first night was a good one. But after that, fever came on. The violent shocks I had been through brought on cerebral congestion, and I knew nothing further for some days.

When I came to myself, I found my mother at my bedside. She had been with me for a week, though I had not known her. After that my arm was treated to more purpose. It was necessary to operate several times. As soon as I was able to be out, I was loaded with invitations. All my nurses asked me to their homes, likewise the doctor, whom I had completely won over, it seems, by the very learned character of my divagations when I was off my head. I have come back to a life of perpetual pampering, sweet, active, calm, and unspeakably happy.

My arm is in a plaster cast. I am writing with my left hand. My room opens out on a large garden, full of flowers and fragrance. I have got back to my books again, and I am growing stronger. To be alive is infinitely good.

June 25. This morning I was decorated with the *Croix de*

Guerre. For several days back my nurses have been going around with an air of mystery. They looked at me and whispered, and for all answer to my questions, did nothing but smile. They had become perfectly inscrutable. Even the doctor, who plied me with his usual volley of jokes, refused to enlighten me. Not until his visit of this morning, did he deign to inform me that the general in charge of this section was going to take the trouble to bring me something.

In the courtyard of the hospital, with its chestnut trees in blossom, and its decorations of flags, were assembled all the wounded who were able to be about, some seated, others lying in reclining-chairs. The ladies in charge of the hospital and all the nurses in their fresh white uniforms were laughing and talking. I was talking to a comrade and feeling not a little embarrassed.

Finally, the general arrived, together with several staff officers. The doctor presented the hospital staff to him and then he presented me. By way of a right arm, I had a big bundle of plaster and bandages which prevented me from being properly clad in my regimentals. The general unfolded a large paper and read in the midst of complete silence:—

Second Lieutenant R. N., the Army cites you in the Order of the Day for the following reasons:—

Lieutenant N., under a very deadly fire, led forward his section to the charge upon the German positions. With great gallantry, he pushed on with his men to a point in advance of the third German line, where he was wounded.

And the general came toward me as I stood there trembling a little, and pinned to my jacket the *Croix de Guerre*. Then he took my left hand and pressed it silently. I felt that everybody was looking at me. I was very much overcome. I must have looked foolish.

The doctor, a sort of demi-god whom we all adore, began to say something. It was about me, doubtless, but I had not the least idea what. I longed for the whole thing to be over. He came up to me and embraced me.

After that we went to the house of the directress and drank champagne. It all seemed endless, and my one wish was to be alone, quite alone, so as to give myself up to the immense, prodigious joy that was mine, the joy that came as a reward for doing my duty. How can I endure this waiting to get well? I must get back to the front. I will prove to my country that not in vain does she reward her children.